THE JAPANESE WORKING MAN
What Choice? What Reward?

7-10-80

The Japanese Working Man:

What Choice? What Reward?

by Ernest van Helvoort

University of British Columbia Press
Vancouver

THE JAPANESE WORKING MAN

©Ernest van Helvoort 1979
Published by The University of British Columbia Press
For sale only in North America

ISBN 0-7748-0109-3

Canadian Shared Cataloguing in Publication Data

Helvoort, Ernest van, 1941-
    The Japanese Working Man

    Bibliography: p.
    ISBN 0-7748-0109-3

1. Labor & laboring classes — Japan
2. Japan — Economic conditions — 1945-
I. Title
HD8726.5.H44   331.1'1'0952   C79-091022-5

Printed in England

2116222

TO MY PARENTS

ACKNOWLEDGMENTS

A volume such as this cannot be put together but with the co-operation of great numbers of great people. Offering my sincere excuses to all those whom I cannot mention at this point, I want to name some whose exceptional support has helped me to see the project through. In Japan, it is Professor Shin-ichi Takezawa (of Rikkyo University) who with great patience and endurance has given the best of his friendship and guidance. Also Professor Yoshitaka Fujita (of Asia University), Mr Kenji Okuda (of Japan Steel and Tube Corporation) and Mr Tsuneo Ono (of the Japan Institute of Labour) have more than indebted me with their suggestions and assistance. In The Netherlands, the help offered by Professors G. Brenninkmeyer and J. Vollebergh has been of great value. I want to thank my previous employer (Nijmegen University, in particular the Department of Psychology) for enabling me, in a multitude of ways, to complete this work before embarking upon a totally different course. Mrs Wies Cloosterman and Mrs Ilse Schipper have rendered invaluable service in typing most of the texts. Mr Paul Norbury and Mrs Micheline Orde have proved irreplaceable in moulding the originally very extensive manuscript into more manageable (and readable, I trust) proportions. Finally, I want to express my gratitude to all those in Japan and in The Netherlands who with their friendship and personal warmth have accompanied me on the way to this—the end result. I hope the book will also encourage the reader to share my fascination with Japan.

Amsterdam, 11 March, 1978   *ERNEST J. VAN HELVOORT*

CONTENTS

FOREWORD

'What has made Japan so successful?', is one of the questions being asked now more frequently than ever. From the total shambles of war, Japan has re-emerged to become an industrial giant in the free world, second only to the USA. With the dawning of the 1970s, more and more accusations were levelled against Japan: exporting inflation, dumping on foreign markets, and undue protectionism in favour of fledgling industries.

In spite of numerous government pledges for appropriate measures to be taken so that growing trade imbalances could be largely redressed, Japan continued to export far more to, than she had imported from, most of her partners. Finally, in 1977/78 her major partners decided to take more forceful action: the Australians in their effort to regain and enhance their position as providers of meat and beef; the Americans in a rather blunt government to government exchange where the US side repeatedly used the threat of selective protectionist measures against Japanese products; and the European Community in similar high-level pressures (though the Japanese seemed far less impressed with the European complaints than with the American ones). At any rate: over the years Japan has managed to build up a position of remarkable strength in the international scene, to the extent that the surplus in her balance of trade with most major partners has become an embarrassment for Japan herself and a source of considerable irritation for the receiving end of Japan's soaring exports.

Once more: what has made Japan so successful in its endeavour to secure a firm hold on the international market place? A great number of 'explanations' have been put forward over the past two decades or so, most of them containing some truth but certainly failing to be totally satisfactory.

One such explanation points out how the West (most notably the USA) has for years allowed the Japanese to buy knowhow, often at low cost, in enormous quantities (until about 1970, as the concept of Japan as a serious competitor began to dawn). Thus, the Japanese were able to gain possession of the most advanced and most efficient technology at relatively low cost, and to gradually build an edge over even those economies where this technology originated—but had not (yet) been widely applied because of a reluctance to scrap gradually outdated plants and machineries.

A related explanation points more specifically to a supposedly unique knack to imitate with-improvements (—not so uniquely Japanese, maybe: the Japanese themselves increasingly blame Koreans and Taiwanese for picking their brains and imitating Japanese produce).

A third argument holds that the Japanese, more than any other nation, have shrewdly profiteered from the Korean and Vietnamese wars, which indeed resulted in enormous boosts on order books for important layers of

Japanese industry ('The Japanese won more by staying out of these wars than they ever could have done while waging a war of their own').

A further explanatory effort relates to the fact that the Japanese—ironically, in large part due to American-imposed stipulations in the Constitution—have for years spent only a tiny fraction of their GNP on defence-related expenditures, far less indeed than their American or most European trade partners considered necessary. Rather than diverting such enormous amounts onto defence and armament, the Japanese were able to channel them into industrial and infrastructural development.

Similarly, it is often pointed out that the Japanese aid to developing nations in comparison lags far behind what its nearest competitors contribute, while it is also said that Japan's aid too often is given on the rigid condition that it is to be used to buy Japanese products and services.

On the economic front, there are the ever louder accusations of Japanese dumping practices on foreign markets, and tough actions being taken, or considered, in retaliation; rare indeed is the American or European citizen who would not suspect Japanese trade practices to be probably unfair. And related to this, there are the bitter complaints that the Japanese market, though officially in large part liberalized, in reality is very hard to penetrate, not in the least because of bureaucratic entanglements at government level which in fact and spirit (though not according to the letter) amount to government protection of domestic industry and market. Also it is said that Japanese export industries in fact are heavily government-subsidized, which is thought to result in over-severe competition and extra unemployment abroad.

Finally, there is the value of the Japanese yen which for years was kept at an artificially low level (360 yen to the dollar), in comparison to other major currencies. The 1972 Nixon shock resulted in minor correction against the US dollar, while late 1977 and early 1978 a marked improvement in the yen's value caused serious concern in Tokyo. In spite of actual revaluations in recent years, some feel that the yen will continue to be undervalued as long as a parity of below 200 yen to the US dollar is not reached, which in fact would maintain an extra advantage in international competition.

All these (and similar) explanations certainly reveal part of the truth of why Japan could be so successful. More likely than not, it is the combination of all this, *plus* what is not stressed very often: the *human factor* on which industrial Japan is founded. Discipline and hard work combine with a clever and often inventive usage of new technology, in an effort to outbid the competitor (both domestic and international). It also presupposes a willingness on the part of many Japanese individuals to subdue their private interests in favour of the interests of their company at large.

This, in turn, presupposes quite a remarkable system of personnel management; a system that offers such inducements to the Japanese employee that she or he will feel eager to identify with the company's interest, maybe to the detriment of one's private short-term interests.

That is what this book intends to look into: the way personnel management is being conducted in Japanese enterprises; how people are motivated to render their services; what are the basic principles of reward and promotion; how are training and education conducted, in relation to the industrial scene; what are the particularly Japanese features in decision-making, participation and communication; how quality control and safety practices are realised; how do Japanese unions fit into this total pattern? And as a provoking thread throughout the book there is the underlying question: how does the Japanese individual worker feel about the way he is being dealt with in his company? Is everyone as happy as is often assumed, or are there underdogs here as well? It will appear that 'typical Japanese' personnel management may be quite rewarding for those who rather see themselves as part of a more important whole, willing to sacrifice their private interests for the sake of those of their company (and a majority of Japanese, certainly in larger companies, seem to fit in this category, and can consequently feel quite secure or even happy in their work). However, Japanese personnel management is less geared to meet the aspirations of those who are more individualistically oriented, who—without necessarily being diehard egotists—want to put emphasis on their own personal development, rather than on company interests; for such people, prospects in a Japanese company may indeed be bleak.

The work on this book was started in the early 1970s and largely completed in early 1975 (except for some later readjustments). Many of the original sources were therefore gathered and studied before that traumatic experience of late 1973 with its inescapable aftermath: the Oil Crisis.

Indeed, I was forced to discard substantial portions of my earliest work as having lost much of its relevance (notably an essay on the tremendous labour shortage that plagued Japan in the early 1970s). Yet, with some updating of certain parts, the main outline of the book has remained valid over the years.

This is mostly due to the fact that I have consistently tried to signal *trends* in personnel management rather than to describe in minute detail what sort of administrative practices or devices were (or are) applied. From that point of view, for example, it is more valuable to know the principles underlying remuneration in several layers of Japan's industrial society, and why so, rather than learn exactly how much a certain 'model worker' received in a certain month of a certain year. Similarly, I have refrained from describing the details of welfare provisions offered by any one firm or institution and instead concentrated on looking into the philosophy behind the existing welfare system and its general outlook.

The fact that the Oil Crisis of 1973-74 interfered with my work, has made the completion of this book easier, in a way, rather than harder. To cite an example: while in the early 1970s the acute labour shortage induced many (especially younger) employees to act as if in a rather mobile labour market, I still could not but conclude (at the time) that lifetime employment security as well as commitment on the part of employer and employee remained one of the most characteristic features within Japanese personnel management. It took the aftermath of the Oil Crisis to prove the point, and to once again highlight some very uniquely Japanese practices of personnel management, which had tended to be blurred during the preceding era of serious labour shortage; in early 1978, Japan's officially announced rate of unemployment stood at slightly over 2 per cent, but private estimates held that if Japanese companies would stop honouring the principle of lifetime employment guarantee, this rate might be as high as 5 or 6 per cent, or even more; similarly, in early 1978 there were several reports of company unions accepting significant salary cuts as a means to help their company weather its present financial predicament.

This does not mean that Japanese employers would indefinitely feel obliged to live up to their earlier promise of lifetime employment security for their personnel. Yet, just as—by and large—during the years of acute labour shortage the majority of Japanese employees (in bigger companies) lived up to the commitment to stay with the same company for all one's working years, now employers are trying hard to honour the earlier commitment not to dismiss personnel, in spite of difficult times in certain branches of industry at present (early 1978). Many hard-hit companies have resorted to a total freeze of recruitment of new employees; other firms 'lend' employees temporarily to third companies where orders are plentiful (eg, a large steel producer recently sent a number of workers to a car manufacturing plant, but the workers concerned remained on the payroll of the steel producer). Other measures include a fairly typically Japanese practice: transferring surplus employees to subsidiaries or subcontractors (thus putting part of the burden on other shoulders), or encouraging 'voluntary' early retirement by surplus employees (thus putting part of the burden on the individual's shoulders, be it with some extra compensatory allowance paid in addition to what he would have received under normal retirement conditions).

It is only in the very last straits, if no other way out is possible, that a company resorts to lay-offs or dismissal of its personnel, and in this case everything will be done to find compensatory employment for the victims. The aftermath of the Oil Crisis thus reveals a solid adherence by Japanese employers to the principle of lifetime employment, just like most Japanese employees stuck to their lifetime commitment during the labour shortage years.

Economic realities do force changes within the Japanese pattern of (personnel) management, but adherence to the principles seems to be quite tenacious, while unavoidable 'breaches' will be redressed as soon as the situation will allow it.

The Japanese Working Man, then, was wrought and appears in the turbulent years before and after the Oil Crisis of 1973-74. The turbulence lies reflected in the following pages, but I have tried to describe what seems to me the more basic principles underlying the Japanese employment scene. It is hoped that the book will thus facilitate an understanding of what is happening and lies ahead in this challenging field that, in turn, lies at the core of what made Japan so successful.

Tokyo, March 1978.

INTRODUCTION: 'THE JAPANESE'

Japan has built up an assortment of industrial activities which from a technological point of view can stand comparison with any of its counterparts in the industrialized world. The technology, however, has been implanted and developed in a socio-cultural environment which features a number of uniquely Japanese characteristics. The wide variety of forms and practices that Japanese personnel management has adopted, for example, reveals a number of commonplace characteristics to the non-Japanese observer, but at the same time may startle him with the number of singularly Japanese features. Japanese technology may be familiar enough to most of us, what we do not know or do not understand at all well is the working of the Japanese mind and spirit. Some understanding and insights into what makes the Japanese Japanese and into their socio-cultural environment is essential in any critical analysis of Japan. It is certainly indispensable for a balanced view of Japanese personnel management practices.

If asked to point out the main difference between Japan and Western societies, no doubt the large majority of experts would somehow come up with a reference to the importance of the group in Japan, as compared with the greater emphasis on the individual in the West. Many different expressions might be used, but everyone certainly would agree on the central issue; in the words of psychiatrist Takeo Doi: 'Generally speaking, the Japanese like group action. It is extremely difficult for a Japanese to transcend the group and act independently. The reason would seem to be that a Japanese feels vaguely that it is treacherous to act on his own without considering the group to which he belongs, and feels ashamed, even, at doing something on his own.'[1]

Takie Sugiyama Kebra puts it this way: '... the Japanese are extremely sensitive to and concerned about social interaction and relationships'. And elsewhere she says: '... the individual Japanese is not a self-sufficient, autonomous whole but a fraction constituting a part of the whole. Belongingness is a necessary basis for establishing identity. The unit of action, then, is the group rather than the individual.'[2]

Group-orientedness, no doubt, is one of the main characteristics of Japanese society. In short, it may be described as an inclination among Japanese individuals to attach great value to being a member of one important group, to more or less neglect individual interests if those of the group are felt to be at stake, and to heavily depend on the group for satisfaction of one's most important needs. Contrastingly,[3] Western societies are thought to foster more individualistic tendencies. The West European, even though being a member of a range of groups, will be inclined to give preference to his private interests over those of any of those groups, and to be more self-sufficient or independent when it comes to personal development and need satisfaction.

Takeo Doi refers to the concept of 'amae' as essential for an understanding of Japanese psychology. This 'amae' refers to a deeply felt need of the Japanese to 'be treated warmly', to 'be cuddled', to be included in a sympathetic and understanding environment; an urge to be enwrapped in the protection of a certain group (or relevant individual) from which security, predictability and warmth can be gained. Doi admits that this need is also generally extant in western societies, i.e. during infancy and early childhood years, but—he adds—it is only in Japan that this amae is considered to be normal for adults as well.

Chie Nakane stresses the importance of vertical relations, notably a strong emotional attachment between a superior and a subordinate, exceeding in relevance any ties existing between group members of comparable level. To put the theories of Doi and Nakane together: Japanese adults tend to satisfy their amae need through strong personal ties with superiors (or subordinates) rather than with immediate peers, also in industry. This means, that on the one hand a Japanese must be a member of a relevant group (e.g. a company, or one of its constituent units), but that most satisfaction is to be derived from vertical relations within this group. Nakane puts it like this: 'The vertical relation . . . in Japan becomes the actuating principle in creating cohesion among group members. Because of the overwhelming ascendancy of this vertical orientation, even a set of individuals sharing identical qualifications tend to create a *difference* among themselves. As this is reinforced, an amazingly delicate and intricate system of *ranking* takes shape.' Apart from this ranking, she says elsewhere, 'the characteristics of Japanese enterprise as a social group are, first, that the group is itself family-like and, second, that it pervades even the private lives of its employees . . .'[4]

The leader of a group, on his part, will try and preserve as much harmony as possible to secure the proper working of his group. At the same time, he will try to satisfy each group member's need for *amae* to the fullest extent, realizing that the group can only exist thanks to the individual's dedication to the leader.

Exclusive identification with the goals and interests of one's company are a dire necessity, often unreflected priority being given to company interests over one's own ('Concern for belongingness urges the individual to contribute to the group goal at the expense of his personal interest'. But then, if the interest or goal of the group 'overrides individual interest, it also overrides the interests of other groups unless a coalition is formed . . . Company employees are aware of the keen competition between companies and try to ensure that their own company wins over other companies'.[5] In this connection, sometimes mention is made of collective or group-egoism (totally acceptable) as contrasted with individual egoism (totally rejectable). Competition, often resulting in blunt ruthlessness, thus seems to be one of the passkeys for understanding Japanese behaviour. Those with whom one does not have any sort of special relation (on account of belonging to the same unit; or on account of ceremonial ties, often in view of a shared goal, like in a seller-buyer situation) can be treated without any extra consideration which often leads to quite rude behaviour in situations where anonymity prevails. Chie Nakane makes the following observations: 'The consciousness of 'them' and 'us' is strengthened and aggravated to the point that extreme contrasts in human relations can develop in the same society, and anyone outside 'our' people ceases to be human.[6] Finally it should be added here that competitiveness evaporates as soon as an outside force is perceived as threatening a common interest of two groups that were so far engaged in a deadly competition struggle. In the end this implies indeed the existence of the overquoted 'Japan Incorporated', as soon as international relations gain weight; this is the area of international competition where 'collective egotism flourishes most uninhibitedly,'[7] often in collusion with, or inspired by, leading government circles; no doubt a diehard 'collective egotism' of a magnitude apparently defying the imagination and concepts of decency existing in most other capitals in the world. (In this connection one may be reminded of the fact that Japanese are frequently held to be opportunists; their behaviour being based upon the situation rather than on mere principle as a guideline).

Group egoism, then, is a very common phenomenon in Japanese society. For example, there is the typical Japanese company union which accepts only regular employees of one specific company as its members, neglecting the interests of anyone except its own members.

The inclination on the part of Japanese individuals to long for membership of a viable group, together with the tendency of Japanese groups to guard exclusively their members' interests are reflected in the four most conspicuous features of Japanese personnel management: lifetime employment security, seniority as a base for promotion and remuneration, consensus-based decision-making and enterprise unionism.

The following (first) chapter ventures to look into the emergence of the first of these features: lifetime employment in the Japanese scene.

1. Taken from Takeo Doi: *The Anatomy of Dependence* (Tokyo, etc: Kodansha International Ltd., 1973), p. 54.
2. T. S. Lebra: *Japanese Patterns of Behaviour* (Honolulu: Univ. Press of Hawaii, 1976), pp 2 and 105. The present section will remind the reader of the ideas of David Riesman; to some extent I can go along with their application to Japanese society, but 'inner — and other — directedness' just does not seem sufficient to explain Japanese behaviour. Lebra (p 3) notes the same, saying that what she calls 'social preoccupation' differs from Riesman's 'other directed', 'which is used in a much narrower sense'.
3. 'In Europe and America individualism is nurtured, that is, the part of the individual is clarified to avoid a conflict of human relations and individual virtue is separated from that of others if we presume that virtue is activities. On the other hand, in Japan where individualism has not developed on the scale as in Western countries, there is a tendency to do a job in the unity of group, that is groupism is strong. As individuals cannot do their jobs without assistance of others, group behaviour is preferable in Japan'. Quoted from M. Murayama's article in *Sophia Economic Review*, vol XIX, 2-3, March 1973, p 85.
4. Chie Nakane: *Japanese Society* (London: Weidenfeld and Nicolson, 1970), pp 25 and 19.
5. T. S. Lebra, op. cit., pp 34 and 35.
6. Chie Nakane: *Japanese Society* (Pelican Books, revised edition, 1974), p 24.
7. T. S. Lebra, op. cit., p. 35. Many Japanese were sincerely surprised about the indignation (repeatedly demonstrated in the 1970s in Western nations) regarding the huge trade imbalances existing (cf. the so-called Nixon shocks and the troubles arising in 1977). In their eyes nothing unusual had taken place, as the international activity was a direct continuation of practices within Japan; moreover, had not a number of Western nations behaved in at least as blatant ways, years or even centuries earlier?

Lifetime employment: historical outline 1

As far back as the 17th century, a widely used employment pattern was that of the *oyabun-kobun* where unskilled labourers clustered around labour contractors *(oyabun)* who acted simultaneously as information points, recruiters and general caretakers. These contractors had some permanent underlings *(kobun)* who were subjected to them in a unique blend of lord-vassal and parent-child relationship which accorded absolute power to *oyabun* and demanded absolute obedience of *kobun*. Nowadays, similar work gangs can still be found, particularly in those industries where casual labour is normally employed (like in construction). Criminal gangs *(yakusa)* also seem to be organised on the same lines.

Another employment pattern developed among the craftsmen in the cities of feudal Japan. Here the master *(oyakata)* would in the course of several years teach the secrets of his craft to his followers. The most important characteristics of this oyakata-employment pattern were: resident apprenticeship from an early age, a strictly hierarchical promotion system based upon length of service, total commitment to the master, and assistance in setting up one's own business. Most craftsmen belonged to various craft guilds similar to those existing in mediaeval Europe.

Both patterns of social relations (labour contractors and master craftsmen) survived the Meiji Restoration of 1868[1] and its concomitant upheavals, and several elements of these patterns may still be found in present-day Japan. According to a 1912 work survey in Osaka, for example, merchant apprentices accounted for approximately seven per cent (about 80,000) of the total population. The attrition rate, however, during the long years of training was very high and the prospect of ever becoming established in one's own business exceedingly remote. Even so, the challenge was considered worthwhile by a great many devotees of the craftsmen's world.

Also still present today are the remnants of the old rigid status-classification system which found its origin in the relatively small *samurai* (warrior) class. In the reasonably peaceful era prior to 1868 there was not much fighting for the warrior class to do. Instead, many samurai became bureaucrats but kept their philosophy of *bushido :* complete and exclusive loyalty to their lord. In other words long before industrialization had started there existed a high-status class of bureaucrats, with clerical and managerial abilities, who adhered strictly to a philosophy of mutual exclusive bonds of loyalty to their employers.

A very different situation existed in the agricultural sector. Business connections developed between cities and villages and the increasing commercialization of agriculture produced a differentiation of the peasantry from a collectivity of self-sufficient farm households into richer and poorer strata, that is, those in a position to demand labour from outside and those in a position to supply labour for additional income.[2] In this way the rural society of pre-industrial Japan had already experienced some sort of unstructured labour market in which employers and labourers co-operated on a casual and contractual basis. It was from this huge reservoir that Japan's industry obtained its unskilled manpower (mostly 'womenpower') : people who were accustomed to casual employment, did not anticipate lifetime commitment; they were used to submitting to authority and willing to work hard for meagre financial rewards.

The Meiji dream: To become number one in the world

Japan's industrialization started directly after the Emperor Meiji embarked on a policy of modernization (late 1860s). The main purpose of this momentous decision was to attempt to equal the industrial, military and cultural strengths of the great colonial powers which were encroaching upon Asia at the time. Indeed, the fundamental principle that governed higher education policy in the Meiji period was Japan's determination to catch up with and, if possible, to overtake 'the powers'—whatever the sacrifice involved, however humbling that might be and whatever the expense. Great numbers of western advisers were recruited, industrial plants and processes were established almost overnight and a western-style military machine took shape with equally dramatic speed—convincingly demonstrated with Japan's victory in the Russo-Japanese war (1904-1905).

Between 1878 and 1900, however, Japan's economic structure consisted mainly of light industries, mostly engaged in the production of textiles. After the first world war (during which Japan was an ally of Britain under the 1902 Anglo-Japanese Alliance) and to some extent immediately before it, there was an impressive sudden growth of heavy machinery and chemical industries, reflected in changes in employment patterns. This was underlined by the fact that for the first time in history the ratio of textile workers to all others fell below the 50 per cent level[3] (sometime between 1914-1919).

For government officials a system of *lifetime employment* had been adopted in the early years after modernization. Private industry followed suit before long, but exclusively for managerial and higher white-collar employees. These *shokuin* were from the beginning endowed with special privileges; in addition to lifetime employment, they enjoyed all kinds of fringe benefits and retirement grants. Both their sense of loyalty and the privileges they enjoyed were in line with those of the former samurai.

Very different was the situation of the *koin* (mainly production workers, skilled and unskilled). Since the urban reservoir of manpower for manufacturing plants soon became insufficient, employers had to look for additional personnel from the countryside. Both urban unskilled workers and the rural migrant work force were accustomed to highly mobile employment relationships. No resemblance of lifetime job security was ever offered, neither was there much inclination for employment commitment on the part of the workers. A very high rate of mobility was also characteristic of skilled and semi-skilled labour whose number was relatively small but whose services were in great demand. Gangs of highly skilled workers and their dependents hiring themselves out for specific jobs and moving from plant to plant in search of high wages were a typical feature of this period.

Given the arbitrary working patterns and conditions of the time, it is not surprising that there were attempts made at the end of the 19th century to organize some form of union movement; there were also sporadic strikes and other forms of industrial action. The Japanese government, however, consistently suppressed any organized labour movements of this kind, and made only a few feeble gestures towards improving the worst of working conditions. This combination of suppression and token compassion actually continued throughout the first decades of the 20th century. A well-known early example is the *Public Peace Police Law* of 1900 which virtually outlawed union organization, strikes and other industrial action. The 1911 *Factory Law* (enforced in 1916) went some way to stamping out the worst excesses in working conditions and labour mismanagement. For example, children under 12 were no longer permitted to work and a minimum rest period of 30 minutes was prescribed for a working day of over 10 hours.

In its fight against the high turnover of its labour force, management (from about 1915 onwards) gradually evolved the 'management-family' philosophy: to create an environment that made it easy for workers to work, so that morale would rise and consequently productivity. Many present-day welfare facilities, in fact, date back to that period. Management also extended the privileges of the *shokuin* to the most essential members of the *koin* ranks, skilled workers who would give up their migrant status and instead would undertake to train selected youngsters within the company. Thus around 1930 three main distinctions could be observed among personnel of large enterprises: (1) shokuin (managerial and higher administrative personnel); (2) koin with lifetime employment and other privileges; (3) koin without lifetime employment and only entitled to the ordinary welfare programme available to all employees. Smaller firms could not afford to offer even remotely comparable conditions of security and related privileges.

It is worth noting that—certainly during the first years of the new 'management familyism'—unions strongly objected to this form of 'paternalism'. For example, *Yuaikai* (The Japan Friendly Society of Labour Federations) issued the following criticism in a 1915 publication: 'In as much as the worker's lot under paternalistic management is entirely dependent on the character and intentions of individual capitalists, paternalism can never be a sure guarantee of workers' well-being. Paternalism or not, workers need labour unions'.[4] And another statement by the same (rather moderate) labour organization said that 'paternalism is a glossover designed to mollify workers', and 'workers do not expect charity of employers. All they are asking for is recognition of their natural rights'.

An additional explanation for this rejection by labour organizations may be found in the fact that a major driving force in the (trade) unions were the craftsmen and labour contractors who were to lose their profitable grip upon the skilled labour market and their virtual monopoly as 'free lance' industrial trainers. It was also a fact that the actual application of the 'management familyism' principle often turned out to be very stringent, with ruthless elimination of 'undesirable' individuals and the absolute demand for workers to obey any orders from their superiors unconditionally.

Through this system big firms found themselves with an employment ace card up their sleeve: they succeeded in obtaining and preserving a highly skilled and stable work force enjoying employment security, relatively high financial rewards, etc. Having lost its right to dismiss these regular employees at will, management created a buffer zone of temporary employees and subcontracting firms to whom risks could be delegated: this was the origin of what is still known as the *dual structure* of Japan's industrial society.

Union oppression in the 1930s

In spite of union resistance, the paternalistic family system of labour relations became widespread in Japanese industry; the dual employment structure also took on ever more definite forms. With the advent of the militarist regime in the 1930s, the oppression of labour organizations became really vehement, virtually eliminating organized labour as a socio-economic partner. The militarist administration strengthened its grip upon society, gearing up the total industrial capacity for war-related production. The concept of the company as a united family was certainly appropriate for early militarist propaganda which stressed this idea explicitly: the company president was the family head and the employees his sons and daughters, while in turn the Emperor was at the apex of the nation at large, the head of all these family heads. Once the militarists had taken hold of the nation, a broad spectrum of laws and ordinances was passed to regulate labour-management relations and virtually everything else. Further regulations affecting working conditions were issued by the militarists concerning recruitment, remuneration, occupational mobility, etc, etc. Workers' food, clothes and even housing depended more than ever on the government and employers, with rationing being organised at places of work.[5] Monthly salary payments were extended to the lower layers of Japan's socio-economic structure. A seniority and cost of living-based remuneration system was devised for everybody, on the premise that every Japanese would contribute his utmost to the realization of his organization's objectives and through those to the goals of the nation. Financial or other rewards should not be based upon individual contribution but should merely serve to sustain the capacity to work on the part of the individual and his dependents. Individual incentive plans thus became totally taboo. All industrial personnel became a member of the only existing 'labour organization' *Sanpo* (Association for Service to the State through Industry) which was organized through separate units ('unions') in most enterprises. Large numbers of personnel were reallocated to war industries and many existing bonds of loyalty were broken. Thus, the privileged position of the happy few under the earlier 'management-familyism' situation was rapidly eliminated during the militarist regime, especially during the war, the distinction between *shokuin* and *koin* being greatly reduced.

Post-war industrial relations

Since the paternalistic family-system of management had virtually ceased to exist by the end of the Pacific War, this was not an explicit point of defiance for the immediate post-war labour movement. On the contrary: in part it even served as a model for postwar industrial relations.

The Japanese nation emerged from the war in total shambles. Prospects were extremely gloomy, with tremendous inflation and widespread unemployment ranking high among the myriad of problems facing the nation. Not only had important elements of her industrial capacity been destroyed, the SCAP (Supreme Commander Allied Powers) authorities also ordered the former *zaibatsu* (giant conglomerates, backbones of Japan's war machinery) to be dismantled. In addition there were those who returned from the battlefields and colonial territories—without employment, since both the armed forces and the colonies had ceased to exist.

One of the initial policies of the SCAP occupation authorities was to encourage the formation of labour organizations as part of the process towards the democratization of Japan. Unions sprang up everywhere reaching an all-time high in 1949. Under the dismal circumstances of the first post-war years, the now powerful unions ventured to demand job security and all sorts of welfare provisions for *all* employees. The prewar practice (as usual under 'management-familyism') therefore functioned as a model for setting up a new labour-relations system, with the important difference that by now job security, or even lifetime employment security, was claimed to be an inherent right of the working population as a whole, not just a generous gift from management to a select part of the labour force.

At first, employers themselves took hardly any direct initiative over the demands that were made by the unions. Many of their leaders had been purged by the allied occupation authorities, and generally speaking, they had lost self-confidence as well as trust from the labour side. In some cases where management did not want to yield to workers' demands, factories were taken over from management by labour groups. It has been written, for example, that after the war Nissan's management had little interest in reconstructing the company and that it was '. . . impoverished workers who took on the task of putting the assembly lines back in operation for the sake of their own subsistence'.[6] Until the outbreak of the Korean War, therefore, workers thus accummulated tremendous power as real promoters of production activities, even occasionally organizing militant offensives against company management.

Besides all this, the first years after the war were characterized by broad egalitarianism and democratization drives, while the Japanese government pushed hard for—at least on the surface—full employment. As a consequence, enterprises were pressed to employ many more people than necessary for production purposes. The unions' demands for lifetime employment security as an inherent labour right actually implied a denial of management prerogatives to adjust the volume of employment through dismissals. Almost everybody received financial remunerations (and often wages in kind) based on the cost of living and family responsibilities (a direct continuation of wartime practices) and barely any trace could be found of the prewar status gap between blue-collar and high-status regular employees. One point should be noted, however: while large companies fared not too badly in the first years after the war, small and medium-sized firms were hard pressed to guarantee lifetime employment or—at least—to realize an eventual promise in that direction. Thus with an enormous surplus of manpower in the first postwar years big firms once again gained the strongest position and could attract the best candidates.

Emergence of 'enterprise-based' unions

Soon, however, the climate in which union power had expanded tremendously (encouraged by the Occupation forces as part of the democratization process) was changed dramatically while management could reconsolidate its position. In 1947-1948, the Dodge economic stabilization plan was implemented to halt economic stagnation. Moreover, the allied occupation authorities who were faced with worrying developments on the Asian Continent (eventually leading to the Korean War, 1949-53) decided not only to favour the industrial recovery of Japan, but to curb the ever-increasing influence of labour unions. The Supreme Commander Allied Powers even ordered the removal of undesirable (leftist) elements from the main industrial labour force (the so-called 'Red Purge'). Under this pretext, large numbers of people were actually discharged, while the Dodge Plan enabled employers to close down unprofitable establishments.

On top of all this the Korean war provided Japanese industry with highly profitable business opportunities; industrialists seized them with both hands: investments soared, unemployment rates plunged down almost out of sight. Management emerged in a very dominant position indeed and soon succeeded in limiting lifetime employment security to only part of the work force: viz all managerial and most white-collar personnel and those blue-collar workers who would be indispensable for the company's operation. Still, compared with prewar practice this meant that considerably more blue-collar workers were to enjoy lifetime security. Meanwhile, management would be free to hire and fire any number of *additional* workers: the union would not include these temporary workers in its membership, nor would it bother too much about their working conditions as long as management would guarantee employment to all 'regular' employees from whom the union would draw its membership exclusively. This is the origin of the present exclusive enterprise-based union.

It must be stressed that the high-status regular work force in large firms could only be maintained at the expense of temporary workers and sub-contracted workers: job security is quite exceptional or virtually non-existent in the lowest part of Japan's dual structure where high turnover and bankruptcies are quite common.

Conclusion

As Shin-ichi Takezawa has said: 'Several years after the end of World War II, implicit consensus emerged among labour, management and government leaders, despite their apparent serious confrontations, on the goal of the nation and the means of achieving that goal'. The goal was both very simple and seductive : namely to achieve the same standards of living as the advanced nations in the West. The decision on the means of so doing involved additional quarrels, but in the end . . . 'a form of division of work developed among the three parties. Management assumed the primary responsibility for productivity improvement, labour would share the productivity gain through collective bargaining, and the government would pave the road for the other parties to play their respective roles'.

Management, therefore, has never officially recognized lifetime employment as an inherent right, even though by this time it has been customary, in one form or another, for nearly 100 years. More importantly, management made it its business to guarantee job security for key personnel, while exercising the prerogative of adjusting employment ratios by other means, such as internal transfers, specific recruitment plans, and discharging at will any or all workers who had not been granted regular employee status. In this sense, the high-status regular work force in large firms today can only be maintained at the expense of the temporary and sub-contracted workers. Enterprise-based unions have confirmed this practice while exclusively admitting regular employees as their members. With the extraordinary economic expansion of the 1960s and early 1970s, more and more smaller enterprises were able to offer some form of lifetime employment guarantee to their key personnel, but job security was and still is quite exceptional or virtually non-existent in the lowest part of Japan's dual structure.

As will be demonstrated in detail later, the implications of the lifetime employment guarantee for the individual are all-embracing, e.g., length of service becomes a significant criterion for employee differentiation ; the employee must readily accept transfers within the firm and orders to perform different duties ; the promotion system must be such that harmony can be preserved among the long-standing manpower force ; selection of employees is crucial since dismissal is next to impossible and school-leavers are preferred to applicants with previous experience because they can be more easily moulded into desirable personalities.

1. The year 1868 marked the completion of a long process during which actual power was returned to the Imperial Throne after a period of usurpation by the *Shogun* (caretaker-generals). The 200-odd years before 1868 are often referred to as 'Edo period' or 'Tokugawa period' or 'Japan's feudal era'. The switch of power in 1868 is usually called the 'Meiji restoration'.

2. Taira K. *Economic development and the labor market in Japan* (New York, London : Columbia University Press, 1970), p. 102.

3. Whitehill A. and Takezawa S. *The other worker—a comparative study of industrial relations in the United States and Japan* (Honolulu : East-West Center Press, 1968), p. 73.

4. Okuda K. Managerial evolution in Japan, III. *Management Japan,* 6, no. 1, 1972, 28-35.

5. Whitehill A. and Takezawa S. *The other worker—a comparative study of industrial relations in the United States and Japan* (Honolulu : East-West Center Press, 1968), 77-8. See also Maruyama M. *Thoughts and behaviour in Japanese politics* (Oxford, etc ; Oxford University Press, 1969), 49-50 ; 363 ; 383-4.

6. Matsuo K. *AMPO—A report on the Japanese People's movements,* no. 20, Spring 1974, p 40.

7. Takezawa S. Changing worker values and their policy implications in Japan. Mimeographed article, New York, 1972. Also published in : Davis L. E. and Cherns A. B. eds *The quality of working life, volume 1* (New York : Free Press, 1975).

The employment paradox 2

The 'regular employee'

The first and most privileged category among Japanese employees consists of what we could call *regular employees*: those employees of larger (and some smaller) firms who work under a contract in which no specific term of employment is mentioned. As a matter of fact, it is against the law to specify an employment duration of more than one year in a labour contract. A guarantee of lifetime employment is based upon social habit, as we have just noted, not upon an explicit written confirmation by management. However, the Labour Standards Law sets down quite stringent rulings in an attempt to protect the employee's right to work. If an employer, for example, wants to dismiss a *regular* employee (the category is important), he must give at least 30 days' advance notice. Other rulings have specified that 'it is an abuse of the employer's right to dismiss workers if the employer cannot produce enough justification for dismissal to persuade the court of its necessity'.[1]

The Labour Standards Law is also very explicit concerning its stipulations over the right of collective bargaining for regular employees in private enterprises, as well as their right to organize unions. In real practice today, the typical Japanese company-based union only accepts as its members individual employees who have attained the status of 'regular employee'.

Within the total group of regular employees a significant criterion for classification is utilized and has to be mentioned here: the level of educational attainment before employment. As Okamoto states: 'The distinctive and rather fixed categorization of employees by educational levels provides a clear contrast with the West where the categorization of equal importance in manpower administration is based on occupational specialization. Given the rule of permanent employment, it is hardly possible for occupational labour markets to emerge, in the same way that the labour market becomes geared to new school graduates classified by educational levels which are often taken as clues for classifying learning ability and social skills.'[2]

The educational system of Japan consists of three different layers: nine years of compulsory education, including elementary and junior high school, three years of senior high school and normally four years at college or university. One can make parallel distinctions among a company's work force : a largely blue-collar force consisting of former junior high-school leavers ; a group consisting of both blue-collar and usually lower white-collar employees who went to senior high-school, and a group of white-collar university graduates or equivalent (especially graduates of junior colleges and similar institutions of higher professional training) whose activities are concentrated in higher administrative and managerial areas.

One additional distinction among regular employees must be made here : a significant criterion for further subdivision of regular employees is the moment of employment with their present firm. Those who joined directly after leaving their last place of education, obtained the status of regular employees and subsequently never changed loyalties by joining another firm, are widely considered as the ideal type : they represent some kind of *standard* regular employee. On the other hand, those who served one or several employers before joining their present firm, are in a slightly inferior position even though being fully fledged regular employees : one might call them *non-standard* regular employees.

(However, the criterion of 'joining the company directly after leaving school' must be understood with some reservation : contrary to previous practices, young people nowadays can be freely admitted to the status of regular employees after they have 'erroneously' wandered about in order to find their true, lifetime company. But this degree of freedom is restricted to younger employees only, say till about the age of 25, and subject to definite limits : extensive previous employment experience is something which cannot be tolerated.)

Recent years have brought some leniency towards non-standard regular employees but they are still at a disadvantage when compared with standard regular employees. Certainly they are not as liable to be discharged at management's will as they were in years gone by, their lifetime employment security seems to be quite well guaranteed. Yet, during many of my interviews with personnel managers, I was told repeatedly that such 'half-way recruits' are very likely to face discrimination when compared with standard regular employees of the same age and school background ; even if their direct financial remuneration and related allowances or fringe benefits are consistent with those of standard regular employees, they will certainly be at a disadvantage as far as their promotion chances are concerned. This means that, among production workers for example, most controlling or supervisory positions are to be occupied by standard regular employees from whose ranks the *core group of employees* is almost exclusively drawn. This core group consists of a certain small proportion of a particular year group, whose career prospects are better than those of their contemporaries. The first selection for membership of this core group takes place during the earliest years of employment. One of the first criteria for their choice is 'proven dedication' and rare it seems that a 'non-standard' regular employee passes this crucial selection.

Japan's new 'middle class' workers

No account is complete without mentioning the 'sarariman' phenomenon. The sarariman (or salaryman; originally referring to those who received salaries instead of wages) does not constitute a distinct employee category: it is a word which carries some very explicit emotional connotations, though slightly leaning towards the negative side; it points to an attitude rather than to a definite group, and it refers to an important segment of Japan's new Middle Class. With the abolition of samurai class distinctions in early Meiji Japan, many ex-samurai became white-collar workers in government offices and government-sponsored industry. As Ezra Vogel points out, 'the similarity between the samurai administrator and the salary man has led many Japanese to refer to the salary man as the modern samurai. His briefcase is compared to the samurai's sword, his company with the feudal fief, his readiness to uphold his company's interests with the samurai's readiness to do battle for his feudal lord. But the salary man is the product of a different social setting . . . being part of a large bureaucratic organization (he) is more concerned with complex administrative and technical problems, has less room for independent movement, and is likely to be more cautious and susceptible to influence'.[3] An important proportion of all *sarariman* are regular employees in big enterprises. Their number seems to be increasing, their pattern of behaviour spreading to other groups as well. In fact, many blue-collar parents dream of their son becoming a *sarariman*. The end of this process is what could be called the formation in Japanese society of a broad 'grey-collar' stratum, one manifestation of which is the strong desire on the part of many non-regular workers to obtain the status of regular employee in a large enterprise.

Chie Nakane states[4] that the structure of the typical middle-class Japanese family is based on a central core: mother and children. The husband has very few social obligations as the household head and finds it all the easier to concentrate his attention on the affairs of his place of work. A man's attention to his wife and children decreases as he climbs the promotion ladder and becomes more involved in the affairs of his firm—and the after-hours visits to bars and restaurants.

Most blue-collar regular employees, however, appear to attach more importance to their family than do their white-collar colleagues for whom unconditional priority of the company seems to be prevalent.

If you are not a 'regular employee', what are you?

Apart from the regular employee group in the larger and medium-sized firms (whether 'standard' or 'non-standard'), there are usually a number of other workers (mainly blue-collar) who are employed on the basis of a short-term but renewable contract: one might call them non-regular employees. This group can be divided into a number of (partially overlapping) categories, such as the *temporary workers,* including *part-time workers,* who have been hired directly by the company under a contract which covers one year at most; *the subcontracted* workers who have been leased to the larger firms by their own smaller company on short term contract; the *seasonal workers,* who leave the farm in winter to earn some additional income; the *day labourers* supplied by labour contractors; the *home workers* mainly supplying a variety of component parts to big industry, and so on.

The Labour Standards Law, which also covers all non-regular employees, is quite specific about the duration of hire and discharge of 'additional' workers. Their term of employment, for example, cannot exceed one year. The usual requirement of 30 days' advance notice for terminating a contract does not have to be met if the labour contract is only for a maximum of two months, or four months seasonal work, or for employment on a daily basis.

No job security is granted to any of these non-regular workers. On the contrary, theirs is the role of shock-absorbing layers in Japan's dual structure. When personnel reductions are deemed necessary in large firms, the contracts of *temporary or subcontracted workers* are simply not renewed. In other words the job insecurity of non-regular personnel is one of the foundations of the lifetime employment system for the regular employee, along with the greater economic risks that larger firms often pass down to small subcontracting firms. Subcontracted workers do not enter directly into contracts with the main company: they may be regular or non-regular employees of the sub-contracting firm. This latter firm, however, often depends completely on the main firm. (Sometimes one hears of a large company founding a subcontractor only to attract cheap labour, which can be disposed of much more easily than personnel hired directly by the large company.)

As a rule, non-regular employees are not allowed to become members of the company-based union, and it is a rarity for such a union to advocate the interests of temporary or other non-regular workers. They remain 'outside people', a concept which has major implications and emotional undertones within Japanese society. Their working conditions are often different from those of regular personnel and their earnings lower, even though they may be employed for several years without interruption and perform the same work as the regular workers. After years of loyal service, some temporary workers may be admitted as regular employees if they pass a competitive examination for which they need the recommendation of a superior.[5]

While some reports indicate that the number of temporary employees is gradually declining, subcontracted workers are on the increase. Japan's dual economy is characterized by the existence of a myriad of small workshops. Certain streets in Tokyo and Osaka consist almost exclusively of small industrial undertakings where, it seems, people are working day and night. It is hard to imagine that these places (frequently badly lit and ventilated) probably have direct connections with some giant industrial concern. Small firms will take great pains to gain subcontracting orders from large firms that in turn will be inclined to delegate to a great number of minor firms any kind of jobs which are menial, involve intensive manpower use or are risky for any other reason. Subcontracting through several levels is a common phenomenon. In this way great numbers of Japanese actually work under some form of subcontracting relationship. There are, of course, some outside workers with special skills who are better paid than regular employees but most are badly underpaid.[6]

The position of most *seasonal workers* in industrial areas is very difficult. With the general housing shortage they have great problems in finding any accommodation; job protection is virtually non-existent. Yet they remain one of the most important buffer groups for the mechanism of supply and demand in the labour market.

Day labourers (of whom many are seasonal workers) form the very bottom of Japan's industrial hierarchy. They are the first to be hit in time of economic crisis and have to take on dangerous or dirty jobs that nobody else wants. In the countryside, women form a substantial proportion of the day labourers' group, but in the cities, men form the majority. Their problems and sheer rejectable working conditions are most clearly reflected in the urban slums where many of them live.

Slum concentrations are a relatively new phenomenon in Japan. Poverty used to be spread evenly over the cities, but with the tremendously increased employment chances there has been a tendency for all kinds of dropouts to gather in certain specific areas. Quite a few of these people belong to the still badly discriminated members of the former Eta-caste, many others are either bankrupt farmers, handicapped war veterans or coal miners driven out of work as oil came to replace coal as fuel in the 1950s. Many day labourers in these slums suffer from diseases associated with alcoholism and the miserable housing conditions facilitate the spread of disease.

During the 1960s the day labourers' ranks were swelled by young farmers who were driven off the farms as a result of the agricultural rationalization programmes in the late 1950s. The 1960s also saw a substantial number of huge construction projects which demanded vast numbers of day labourers and included the building of the Shinkansen (Bullet Train) railway from Tokyo to Kyoto, the 1964 Tokyo Olympics and the 1970 Osaka World Exposition.

Today Tokyo has about ten slum areas, the biggest being Sanya. The biggest concentration of all, however, is in Osaka's Airin (Neighbourly Love) district. There are other sizeable concentrations in Yokohama, Fukuoka, Kagoshima and Sapporo.

The average age of the day labourers in the slums is slightly over 30, most of them being male and only about 1 per cent married. Many of them do not have houses or rooms, they just rent a bed for the night; in some cases night workers rent for daytime, enabling certain landlords to earn twice as much as they would normally. Compared with permanently employed workers their wages are mostly very low and they have to rely heavily on overtime to be able to make a living.

Black-market labour pushers must be mentioned here. Inevitably, as elsewhere in the world, the supply of such labour is heavily dominated by underworld bosses. In 1973 it was estimated by the Police that 2,500 construction firms were controlled by criminal gangs.

Very strong prejudices (or indifference at best) towards the slums' day labourers and their conditions prevail in Japan today. At best most Japanese seem to be inclined to consider these people as 'a psychiatric problem' or 'a police problem', rather than to see them as a social problem of the nation as a whole or even as a sad consequence of the exclusive group orientation of Japanese society. A writer to the *Japan Times* once remarked bitterly: '... rather than making determined efforts to correct a given situation by facing the facts and probing into the depths of the problem, Japanese have the tendency always of 'passing the buck' to someone else to make them shoulder the consequences of any abnormality of situation created, so that the provision of a scapegoat became a necessary corollary for the perpetuation of Japanese society'.[7]

As regards the foreign blue-collar worker in Japan, before and during the Pacific War many Koreans were forced to lend their services to Japanese industry where they had to work under unbelievably bad conditions. The same was true of working conditions in the then colony of Korea herself. Today, there are still many Korean families residing in Japan and often enough these are faced with severe discrimination, in employment as well as in other fields.

Japan's working population

The question now arises as to how many workers belong to the category of regular employees and how many to the category of non-regular employees. The Ministry of Labour offers some estimates, using the following definitions: a *regular employee* has a contract of employment without a specified period of employment or (in some cases) with a period of more than one year (officials of companies and associations are also included); *temporary employees* are employed for a month or more but not more than a year; *day labourers* are employed on a daily basis or for a specified period of less than a month; *self-employed workers with paid employees* own and operate unincorporated enterprises, usually employing one or more paid employees; *self-employed workers who do not employ any paid workers* and who operate their business alone or with unpaid family workers; *family workers* who work in an unincorporated enterprise operated by a member of the family.

The table overleaf gives an approximate idea of the number employed in each category. According to this table about 64 per cent of all employees (almost 80 per cent in manufacturing) are covered under lifetime-employment security conditions, but this seems to be an exaggeration, or at least should be interpreted with care. Included are numerous employees in small firms who admittedly work under a contract without a specified period of employment, but who in reality are not too certain about their job security. Neither do many of them show any serious intention of lifetime commitment for which the firm rewards them with yearly increasing seniority-related pay increments till retirement. In addition the Ministry of Labour includes numerous part-time and full-time *female* workers whose conditions of work, remuneration, promotion, fringe benefits, etc. are vastly inferior to those of the male standard regular employee in large firms (see next chapter). All in all, the group of regular employees (in a strict sense) who do enjoy lifetime employment and related privileges in my estimate does not exceed half of those concerned, probably even being not more than about 40 per cent of the total working population.

2116222

Table 1

EMPLOYED PERSONS BY INDUSTRY, STATUS AND TYPE OF EMPLOYMENT, 1970, 1972 AND 1975

(numbers × 1,000)

Industry	Year	*Total	Regular Employees	Temporary Employees	Day Labourers	†Self-Employed	Family Workers
All industries covered	1970	50,940	30,230	1,650	1,180	9,770	8,050
	1972	51,090	31,500	1,780	1,240	9,460	7,060
	1975	52,230	33,460	1,770	1,230	9,390	6,280
Agriculture and forestry	1970	8,420	170	30	90	3,630	4,510
	1972	7,050	170	30	70	3,240	3,550
	1975	6,180	190	30	70	3,020	2,860
Fisheries and aquaculture	1970	440	150	20	10	150	110
	1972	490	170	10	10	170	120
	1975	430	160	10	—	160	100
Mining	1970	200	170	10	10	10	10
	1972	160	140	10	10	—	—
	1975	160	150	—	—	—	—
Construction	1970	3,940	2,250	240	560	690	200
	1972	4,310	2,550	270	590	710	190
	1975	4,780	2,980	230	560	800	220
Manufacturing	1970	13,770	10,570	630	240	1,490	850
	1972	13,780	10,680	610	220	1,480	790
	1975	13,650	10,630	530	220	1,360	720
Wholesale, retail, finance, insurance and real estate	1970	11,440	6,870	340	110	2,260	1,860
	1972	11,970	7,270	400	120	2,310	1,860
	1975	12,970	8,060	470	160	2,440	1,860
Transportation, communication, electricity, gas and water	1970	3,530	3,270	90	40	100	30
	1972	3,540	3,270	90	30	120	30
	1975	3,640	3,340	90	40	140	40
Services	1970	7,510	5,220	260	100	1,430	490
	1972	7,970	5,600	310	120	1,420	510
	1975	8,550	6,090	360	130	1,460	500
Government	1970	1,610	1,140	40	30	—	—
	1972	1,750	1,630	50	60	—	—
	1975	1,960	1,850	50	50	—	—

Sources:
Yearbook of Labour Statistics 1970 (Tokyo: Ministry of Labour, 1971), p.12.
Yearbook of Labour Statistics 1972 (Tokyo: Ministry of Labour, 1973), 10-1.
Yearbook of Labour Statistics 1975 (Tokyo: Ministry of Labour, 1976), 10-1.

*Note. There are some minor flaws in the original statistical material, e.g. counting up subtotals one may find slightly different results. Since the above numbers are close estimates, these minor discrepancies should not prevent the reader from obtaining the information essentially desired.

†Both categories of self-employed workers, as defined by the Ministry (see above).

1. *Japan Labor Bull.,* May 1, 1970, p.8.

2. *Japan Labor Bull.,* Oct 1, 1970, p.6.

3. Vogel E. F. *Japan's new middle class—the salary man and his family in a Tokyo suburb* (Berkeley: University of California Press, 1971), p. 5. I use the 'sarariman' spelling as it comes closest to the Japanese pronunciation.

4. E.g. see her well known *Japanese Society* (London: Weidenfeld and Nicolson, 1970), p. 157.

5. Many companies consider all their new regular-employees-to-be as temporary personnel, for the duration of the usual probation period. Even though some of these probationers may not pass the test, by far the great majority easily moves up into the ranks of the regulars. Those who belong to the category of 'real' temporary employees have much greater trouble to become 'regular'.

6. The National Union of General Workers (Zenkoku Ippan) must be mentioned here: it rejects the principle of the company-based union and accepts only individual workers ('outside people') as its members; in a way, it is intended as a haven for those who are denied membership in a company union. So far, however, its influence has been very limited.

7. *The Japan Times,* January 16, 1972.

Working women, homeworkers and handicapped employees

Working women in Japan

The usual personnel management practices concerning women specifically, will only occasionally be dealt with in this book, often indirectly as well. Just like personnel management itself in Japanese industry still seems to be geared to male employees, this book shows a similar bias. Therefore it seems useful to pay special attention to female employees first, however briefly.

Between 1960 and 1970, the number of working women in Japan more than doubled. In 1975 there were over 43.4 million women of employable age (15 years and older; as compared to about 41.1 million men), of whom 45.8 per cent actually participated in the labour force (males 81.3 per cent), which corresponded to slightly over one third of the gainfully employed population.

Since 1967 there has been a steady decline in female labour-force participation (1967, 51.2%; 1972, 47.8%; 1973, 48.2%; 1974, 46.6%; 1975, 45.8%; note the rather sharp drop after the oil crisis of late 1973, which apparently resulted in relatively less women being employed).

In 1960 only 37 per cent of all employed women were married: by the early 1970s the ratio had increased to more than 50 per cent. In 1973 60 per cent of all females above the age of 60 were working: many of these older women working as part-time employees. In 1970 the total number of part-time workers was estimated at 2.5 million throughout the nation and almost 90 per cent of these were female.

Some female full-time or part-time employees are granted the status of regular employee, but in most cases, even if they are employed for an indefinite period of time, this implies that they are actually considered and treated as temporary workers, to be trusted with low-skill and low-responsibility jobs. Government statistics confirm that most firms employing women use them primarily in production processes or for simple clerical administration and sales duties. For the most part the female employee is only asked to undertake simple work with a minimum of responsibility—despite the relatively high (and improving) levels of education of women in Japan. Prospects of in-service training in industry and commerce are also remote. The few graduate girls employed in industry are normally classified differently from their male colleagues (examination standards tend to be lower among women) and their chances of a career are virtually non-existent. The exceptions are so notable that they are newsworthy. In 1971, for example, Miss A. Takita working for Japan Air Lines in the PR Department became the first woman in Japan to be promoted to the status of manager. She later published a book about her career.

Table 2 provides some extra insight into the number of women employed and the sectors of industry where they work. No separate distinction of 'part-timers' is provided.

Statistically speaking, turnover among female employees is higher than among males, one important factor undoubtedly lying in the fact that there are still many cases where women are expected to resign from a company on marriage or first pregnancy, even though they may not wish to do so and despite the fact that they were employed on a permanent basis as a regular employee in the first instance. A government study on the 'Womanhood of present-day Japan' (May 1974) indicated that most women seem to accept this 'early retirement practice' as a perfectly normal process (even though this attitude seems to be changing). Recent court rulings have clearly indicated that special rules of employment regarding retirement provisions for women, specific criteria that married women are the first to be laid off when business declines, and company pressure on women to retire after marriage, are illegal. 'The courts ruled that such dismissal by agreement or persuasion is in violation of the freedom of marriage and the equality of men and women guaranteed by the Constitution'[1] Despite such rulings a recent government survey on the subject[2] revealed that over 23 per cent of companies questioned (with at least 30 employees) openly enforced specific regulations for the retirement of women employees. Of these firms, about 5.4 per cent required female workers to leave before the age of 35, 4.9 per cent before the age of 40, 16.3 per cent before the age of 46, 32.4 per cent at the age of 50, 25.6 per cent at the age of 55; but virtually no company in the sample required their male employees to retire before the age of 55. It was interesting that during the business boom and labour shortage of the early 1970s some managements were induced to invite female employees (back) to (re)enter employment once their duties at home were mostly finished. Some companies even formulated specific programmes, offering modest 'privileges' to those women prepared to return to their original company.

There is clear evidence of an inverted relation between company size and number of female employees. Not only do relatively more women work in smaller firms, their age also seems to be higher there than in larger companies.

Table 2

EMPLOYED PERSONS BY INDUSTRY, STATUS (AS DEFINED BY THE MINISTRY OF LABOUR) AND TYPE OF EMPLOYMENT: 1975

females (F) and males (M) (numbers × 1,000)

Industry	Sex	Total*	Regular Employees	Temporary Employees	Day Labourers	†Self-Employed	Family Workers
All industries covered	F	19,530	9,950	1,180	540	2,810	5,020
	M	32,690	23,510	590	690	6,590	1,260
Agriculture and Forestry	F	3,230	40	20	30	800	2,350
	M	2,950	150	20	40	2,240	510
Fisheries and aquaculture	F	80	10	—	—	—	60
	M	360	150	10	—	160	40
Mining	F	10	10	—	—	—	—
	M	150	140	—	—	—	—
Construction	F	590	340	50	110	—	100
	M	4,180	2,650	180	450	800	110
Manufacturing	F	4,750	3,070	400	150	570	550
	M	8,710	7,560	130	70	770	160
Wholesale, retail, finance, insurance, and real estate	F	5,830	3,120	370	120	710	1,510
	M	7,130	4,930	100	40	1,720	330
Transportation, communication, electricity, gas and water	F	440	370	40	10	—	20
	M	3,190	2,960	50	30	150	10
Services	F	4,250	2,750	270	100	710	410
	M	4,300	3,340	90	40	750	80
Government	F	310	240	40	30	—	—
	M	1,660	1,610	10	20	—	—

Source: *Yearbook of Labour Statistics 1975* (Tokyo: Ministry of Labour, 1976), 10-1.

*Note: There are some minor flaws in the statistical material, e.g. counting up sub-totals, one may find slightly different results. Since the above numbers are close estimates, these minor discrepancies should not prevent the reader from obtaining the information essentially desired.

†Note: Both categories of self-employed workers, as defined by the Ministry (see before table 1, chapter 2).

Women earn substantially less (see Table 3). While at an early age the wage differences between female and male workers are not very big, after about 30 the gap grows much wider, especially in the larger firms. The wage system for male employees is still largely based on the principle of seniority-based remuneration, but the same principle is widely ignored for female employees over 30 whose earnings may even go down, except in the smallest firms (but there without much progress). These differences are the more conspicuous since all kinds of allowances (including two bonuses a year) are derived from basic monthly earnings, which places men in a very much more favourable position than women (see Table 3).

In spite of all this, such differentials in pay rates do not *directly* contradict the principle of equal pay for equal work (as guaranteed in the post-war Japanese Constitution) but indeed women are mainly assigned to auxiliary work, they retire early and have trouble contributing as much to the company as male employees. Added to this there is a generally held belief that 'real' work is more suitable to men, that the husband has to be the main breadwinner and that the income of the wife can be only supplementary.

Table 3

AVERAGE MONTHLY CONTRACTUAL CASH EARNINGS BY AGE, COMPANY SIZE AND SEX: REGULAR EMPLOYEES (GRADUATES OF ELEMENTARY SCHOOL AND/OR POSTWAR JUNIOR HIGH SCHOOL) JUNE 1975

(in between brackets: bonus amounts received in 1974) (× 1,000 yen)

Age group	Company size	Males		Females	
-17	A=1000-	65.9	(139.1)	60.8	(132.5)
	B= 100-999	65.3	(119.1)	58.9	(108.5)
	C= 10- 99	62.8	(80.7)	56.2	(67.3)
18-19	A=1000-	80.5	(277.1)	68.1	(259.2)
	B= 100-999	74.0	(256.2)	64.2	(206.0)
	C= 10-99	73.4	(185.3)	61.1	(124.9)
20-24	A=1000-	95.1	(381.7)	79.8	(332.6)
	B= 100-999	90.9	(343.3)	70.2	(241.2)
	C= 10-99	91.4	(248.8)	63.2	(141.7)
25-29	A=1000-	115.7	(481.5)	89.5	(390.2)
	B= 100-999	110.8	(439.8)	72.8	(250.7)
	C= 10-99	108.7	(318.4)	61.8	(129.4)
30-34	A=1000-	135.3	(574.3)	90.3	(381.0)
	B= 100-999	127.5	(520.0)	68.6	(209.8)
	C= 10-99	121.8	(371.3)	59.9	(123.7)
35-39	A=1000-	146.5	(626.0)	87.1	(356.5)
	B= 100-999	135.1	(550.1)	68.0	(209.8)
	C= 10-99	124.1	(371.0)	61.6	(138.0)
40-44	A=1000-	155.5	(689.5)	88.6	(367.2)
	B= 100-999	138.2	(572.5)	69.6	(222.2)
	C= 10-99	122.0	(366.8)	61.6	(145.5)
45-49	A=1000-	164.6	(763.6)	91.9	(393.0)
	B= 100-999	136.1	(552.2)	71.2	(232.4)
	C= 10-99	117.3	(354.9)	63.0	(150.5)
50-54	A=1000-	171.2	(807.8)	86.7	(353.1)
	B= 100-999	136.3	(558.2)	72.0	(233.7)
	C= 10-99	115.3	(342.6)	63.3	(156.7)

Source: *Katsuyo Rodo Tokei, 1977 (Compendium of Labour Statistics, 1977)* (Tokyo: Japan Productivity Centre, 1977), p. 69.

One may wonder why Japanese housewives have recently shown a relatively high readiness to seek re-employment: certainly not because of the challenging work, responsibility or high financial rewards awaiting them! Some explanation may be the rapid rising level of living standards, inflation and prices with which the general wage levels have not kept pace. Then there is the fact that the Japanese family has become smaller and women's housework easier due to the spread of electrical domestic appliances which are now commonplace in all Japanese homes. Quite a few Japanese women do not seem to know how to spend their leisure hours once their children are at school, it seems, yet their remaining household obligations prevent them from finding better paid full-time jobs.

The present Labour Standards Law (dating back to 1947) contains a number of protective measures for working women, but it is often said that it is exactly these protective regulations which serve to handicap women in competition with men, since the restrictions on overtime, etc., may obstruct the promotion prospects of women (who stay longer on the job nowadays than some decades ago). Overtime for women on rest days is prohibited and management is forbidden to employ a woman six weeks before and after childbirth. The Labour Standards Law also provides for nursing time and menstruation leaves. It bans, in principle, midnight work for both women and minors between the hours of 10 pm and 5 am, restricts their employment on dangerous and harmful jobs, and prohibits them from working underground in mines.

Women employees are getting more aware of the unequal position they are in: they want to be treated the same way as men, have comparable chances of promotion and appropriate training, at present practically impossible. Some changes seem likely to come but Japanese women may have a long way to go before some semblance of equality is accomplished. Experts feel that the legal provisions should be altered in view of the increasing importance of the female work force in industry. One proposal for revising the protective regulations for women employees was submitted to the Ministry of Labour by the Tokyo Chamber of Commerce and Industry which 'in particular, is of the opinion that much of the special treatment or protective legislation for employed women has become unsuitable in terms of today's improved working environment as well as the much improved physical conditions of working women themselves'.[3] Mainly in view of the then tight employment situation, the following specific suggestions were formulated (and in part drew heavy criticisms): (1) ease the restrictions on overtime work; (2) relax the ban on employment of women for hazardous and injurious jobs; (3) reduce the ban on midnight labour; and (4) delete the article on menstruation leave. Additional proposals regarding modification of the present Labour Standards Law include an extension from six weeks to eight weeks or more for women's maternity leave. The planned new Employment Insurance Bill is expected to call for a special extension of the period during which unemployment benefits can be received by a woman who leaves her job due to pregnancy or childbirth. In addition, during the serious labour shortages around 1970, quite a number of firms have initiated so-called 'infant-care-leave' regulations (especially regarding skilled female workers), through which women could leave work for a certain maximum period (e.g. one year) to take care of a baby and then return to their original jobs.

Several surveys have indicated that female employees display a more contractual attitude to their employer than most male colleagues. Women workers (in a study by Whitehill and Takezawa reported in 1968) 'showed less willingness than men to accept management rules and penalties ... Women generally hold less enviable job status and responsibility than men. It is very likely that the more limited sense of subordination was a reflection of such differences in status and responsibility'.[4] During the decade which followed that study, the number of working women virtually doubled, their length of service also increased significantly, and yet their job status and responsibility remained low when compared with those of men.

A study of my own may be mentioned in this context.[5] Early in 1972, I conducted a questionnaire survey among some 300 rank-and-file young women employees (and a similar number of blue-collar male workers in the same firm) in a large synthetic fibre manufacturing plant. From the men I frequently heard utterances such as 'those women only come to industry to make money, and to gossip with their colleagues'. The women, indeed, were relatively more bothered by the lack of mutual communication possibilities while at work; also they would have preferred the canteen to be cosier, and 'sociability' to be a more important subject for personnel appraisals. But as far as financial remuneration was concerned, the men expressed much stronger dissatisfaction than did the women (about virtually all financial issues). The girls expressed very deep dissatisfaction regarding the possibilities of personal development and self-realization. They felt strongly about the meaninglessness of their work; also about the lack of opportunity for using their initiative together with their own skills and abilities, etc. My findings underline the fact that female workers in Japan are becoming increasingly aware of the unequal position they are in, they want to be treated the same way as men, they want to have some chance for promotion and appropriate training.

Training possibilities for female employees are extremely restricted or—if available—irrelevant, in many companies. A woman who wants to get ahead in industry does not—as seems often to be assumed—primarily need a course in flower arrangement or tea ceremony, while household economics may be a worthwhile topic in itself, but does not serve much purpose for a working woman pursuing an industrial career. A modern, often cited Japanese comment is 'After the Pacific War, three things became stronger: stockings, unions and women!' Ironically, most stockings have been produced by women, while their rate of union organization has been relatively low: e.g., in 1970, only 29.4 per cent of eligible female employees belonged to a union, compared to about 38 per cent of all male workers (these figures had not changed substantially by 1977).

Let me end by recalling an event which made headlines and induced much serious comments not long ago. Women who work in offices in Japan are, as a rule, required to serve green tea to their male colleagues and to visitors several times a day. This is a perfectly normal occurrence in the family as well: women serve tea. Recently there have been some incidents with women refusing to perform this duty any more in their offices, on the premise that such activities are not included in their labour contracts.

Some changes seem to lie ahead, but Japanese women still have a long way to go before some semblance of equality is accomplished.

Homeworkers

A large number of homeworkers are engaged in work entrusted to them by wholesale dealers or manufacturers: most of them are older women and therefore this section is included here. According to government information there are today more than 2 million homeworkers, of which over 90 per cent are female. Many of them make small parts to be assembled later in manufacturing plants. It is well known that the range and output of Japanese industry increased impressively between 1970-74, but so did the homeworkers' jobs; side jobs, for example, related to transportation machinery, electrical equipment, food and ceramics were said to have increased by 167 per cent, 902 per cent and 149 per cent respectively. 'In addition to traditional jobs, including most daily commodities from sewing to craft-work and toy-making, new kinds of side jobs include cutting the edge of parts for automobile press work, making machines for diesel engine fuel pumps, assembling and packing nylon zip-fasteners, making mosaic tiles, coating wire and assembling parts for TV sets and communication instruments.'[6]

Homeworkers worked on average 5.8 hours a day and 21 days a month, compared with slightly over 8 hours and 22.9 days for regular employees (early 1970s). The Industrial Homework Bill (passed in 1970) was intended to deal with the worst of substandard working conditions under which many homeworkers had to operate, but the protective regulations seem to be restricted to the very minimum.

Handicapped employees[7]

The number of physically handicapped people in Japan at present is estimated at about 1.5 million people (almost 60 per cent being handicapped in the use of certain limbs, almost 20 per cent in the use of their eyes, and another almost 20 per cent being handicapped because of deficiencies in hearing, speaking or equilibrium).

In 1960 the Physically Handicapped Persons' Employment Law was first enacted. Among the provisions of this law: private companies were to employ 1.3 per cent of their workforce from among the physically handicapped (compliance to be rewarded with an amount of ¥14.000 per month per handicapped employee; companies in the public sector were to take in up to 1.7 per cent from among the physically handicapped); in addition, companies employing at least this minimum percentage were to receive financial rewards during the first period (maximum 18 months) of employment, per person; establishments employing many physically handicapped persons were entitled to extra financial aid such as loans at favourable conditions and certain tax incentives; the law also provided for workshop training and sheltered workshops.

The record of Japanese industry (regarding employment of physically handicapped people) has been less than admirable. Many handicapped people who possessed abilities and willingness to work had trouble finding decent employment (estimates run from 'at least 10 per cent' till 'about one third'). Late 1976 a number of new regulations came into force, the main ones being: private companies now are to hire at least 1.5 per cent (was 1.3) of their workforce from among the physically handicapped (and will be rewarded if complying), and companies not measuring up to this standard are to pay ¥32.000 per month for 'the lacking number'. The new regulations are likely to have some impact, but it is still too early to judge what their actual result will be. For one thing the amounts involved do not yet seem to be impressive.

1.   *Japan Labour Bull.*, Nov 1 1973, p. 2.

2.   *Katsuyo rodo tokei 1977 (Compendium of labour statistics)* (Tokyo: Japan Productivity Center, 1977), p. 113.

3.   *Japan Labour Bull.*, Dec 1 1970, p. 2.

4.   Whitehill A. and Takezawa S. *The other worker—a comparative study of industrial relations in the United States and Japan* (Honolulu: East-West Center press, 1968), p. 116.

5.   For a more extensive report on this study see my *Blue-collar workers in Japan and Holland: a comparative study* (Meppel-Holland 1977).

6.   According to a report in *AMPO:* A report on the Japanese people's movements (no 18, Autumn 1973, p. 55). This source estimates the number of homeworkers to be far more than the 2 million indicated in government reports.

7.   My coverage (however brief) of handicapped employees may seem out of place in this chapter. I have chosen to insert these paragraphs here as the remainder of this book will scarcely mention them.

Japan's older workforce 4

The elderly: a national predicament?

Many of those who gave their utmost to realize Japan's economic marvel of the last few decades are the ones who at present cause most concern among experts. In the words of Takezawa 'the older generation in their 50s and 60s . . . is by far the most neglected group in industry in present-day Japan'. Shunzo Arai writes '. . . a kind of human inflation has developed in Japan, with the older employees being denied their just paternalistic benefits . . . many of them are confronted with a very bleak predicament and it has become a problem of concern to Japanese society as a whole'.[2]

In the old days, a Japanese elderly couple would live with the family of the oldest son and in that way society took care of the old who were awarded due respect and obedience throughout their lifetime. Modern developments, however, resulted in the eventual separation of the younger generation and the original family which mostly remained in the non-industrialized countryside. Urban housing conditions have prevented children from taking elderly parents in their homes even if they wanted to. Moreover, while formerly a person of 60 or older was quite exceptional in Japan, and therefore was treated with great reverence and respect, the rapidly increased life expectancy has contributed to steadily growing numbers of aged persons and respect seems to have declined as the life expectancy increased. Modern Japan's industrial society has tended to concentrate its interest on those who can be directly productive or hold a promise for the future while the plight of the elderly is cause for increasing concern. This is certainly true in a financial sense.

Earning and age

One only has to look at wage and salary developments over recent years to conclude that middle aged and older workers see the young generation eat away steadily at what they had considered a safe investment for their own future.[3] For example: around 1960, a production worker in a large firm at the start of his career (age 18) could expect to earn three times as much basic salary within ten years, and five times as much in 20 years of service as a beginner in the same company.

By 1975 a production worker in a large firm after ten years of service earned just about twice a beginner's wage and substantially less than three times as much after 20 years. While (again in large firms) a 50 year old production worker in 1961 earned almost 6.5 times a beginner's basic salary, in 1975 he made just about three times as much. This relative decline not only afflicted production workers, but also those engaged in administrative and managerial activities (particularly the university graduates).[4]

Table 4 gives an impression about the monthly contractual cash earnings, as well as annual special cash earnings (bonuses), for several age groups of regular male employees in companies of different sizes, in 1975. In smaller companies, one notices a decline in earnings from about age 45; in middle-sized companies the peak of earnings seems to lie between 45 and 49, while it lies between 50 and 54 in the largest firms. A look at the columns 3 in the table reveals that the older categories of employees have by far their strongest representation in the smallest companies, which indicates that smaller companies are more ready to employ older workers than large firms. Another survey by the Ministry of Labour (in June 1976) found the same thing: out of 12,000 firms sampled, 65 per cent employed older people (age 55 or over) at a rate of less than 6 per cent of their total workforce; 15 per cent at a rate of 6 to 10 per cent; 19 per cent at a rate of 10 to 20 per cent; and 10 per cent at higher rates. Only about one third of larger companies employed 6 per cent or more elderly people, as compared with 65 per cent of companies with less than 100 employees. All this in spite of the recently (1976) revised special 'law for promotion of employment of elderly workers' which recommends that all firms employ older people at a rate of at least 6 per cent.

One explanation for the fact that elderly people are so heavily over-represented in smaller firms is to be found in the so-called age-limit system.

The age-limit system

In Japan for a variety of reasons, four out of every five pensioners have got a job. Most larger companies retire their employees relatively early, usually at 55 and pay them some kind of allowance on that occasion. Then they may rehire them, or at least help them to find a new job, but in such cases financial and other working conditions will most likely be inferior to the pre-retirement situation. Since the Japanese social security system is poor and retirement is early, older employees in Japan have become a relatively cheap labour reserve with great willingness to work (to the advantage of the smaller company particularly).

It is astonishing for many observers that large Japanese companies on the one hand guarantee their regular employees secure

Table 4

TOTAL MONTHLY CASH EARNINGS (1); ANNUAL SPECIAL CASH EARNINGS (2);
AND ESTIMATED NUMBER OF EMPLOYEES (3); SIZE AND AGE GROUPS;
1975; REGULAR EMPLOYEES ONLY

Sample survey of about 60,000 establishments (10 or more regular employees)

Age	1000 employees or more			100-999 employees			10-99 employees		
	1	2	3	1	2	3	1	2	3
	× 1000 yen		× 10 persons	× 1000 yen		× 10 persons	× 1000 yen		× 10 persons
-17	69.0	139.4	1.601	66.0	112.1	3,144	64.8	67.6	3.775
18-19	88.0	155.1	15.801	81.9	133.5	12.614	79.3	102.8	10.516
20-24	105.0	371.8	75.001	101.4	306.0	60.913	100.0	221.0	54.793
25-29	130.8	535.4	111.014	127.4	461.1	88.862	123.2	328.6	83.803
30-34	161.6	698.7	98.495	154.8	596.1	72.150	144.7	422.4	70.046
35-39	184.0	836.6	83.469	172.1	693.0	59.462	153.3	452.2	61.284
40-44	199.3	950.9	72.878	179.0	724.7	49.491	153.4	448.7	54.217
45-49	208.1	1002.8	70.157	180.8	732.3	35.925	151.0	438.9	40.897
50-54	218.6	1080.5	46.610	179.6	736.3	24.248	146.4	428.0	30.035
55-59	202.2	957.7	16.810	157.5	583.3	14.862	131.6	362.0	23.189
60-	159.0	676.1	6.950	129.3	437.5	13.566	115.3	298.3	28.763
Total	165.2	733.6	597.786	146.9	552.6	435.237	133.7	369.4	461.317

Source: *Yearbook of Labour Statistics, 1975* (Tokyo; Ministry of Labour, December 1976), p.120-121.
NOTE
  (1)=total monthly contractual cash earnings × 1,000 (yen)
  (2)=annual special cash earnings × 1,000 (yen)
  (3)=estimated number of male regular employees × 10 (persons)

employment but on the other hand discharge them at a relatively early age. There are several reasons for this practice. First of all, average life expectancy: not until 1947 was the average life expectancy of 50 exceeded, so an age limit of 55 really, at the time, was seen as an advanced age. (In 1975 life expectancy for Japanese males was reported to be 71.76 and females 76.95: now amongst the highest in the world.)

Another reason is to be found in the very nature of the lifetime employment practice itself: to make room for young people, the older employees have to go; moreover an older person's adaptability to innovation and other challenges is likely to decline while his own skill and knowledge tends to become obsolete. Yet under conditions of lifetime employment the man with higher seniority most probably will be entrusted with more responsibility.

Finally, those with highest seniority levels traditionally were (and often still are) entitled to the highest (or at least very high) remuneration levels within their own category: so purely for financial reasons a company also may favour early retirement for many of its older employees. Today many people feel that the prevailing retirement age limit comes too early, that lifetime employment privileges are rather cruelly restricted to the most productive years of one's life.[5]

In many cases it is not possible any more for an elderly couple to move in with the family of the oldest son, as used to be the case traditionally; when they have to leave the company's house on retiring many pensioners will use the lump sum they receive at the moment of separation to buy a house. This introduces the following question : what sort of financial provisions do Japanese firms offer their retiring and retired employees?

Financial provisions for retirement

In spite of recently initiated efforts to create a viable national welfare pension system for the elderly, many (or perhaps most) of Japan's older citizens have to live under the most abysmal circumstances. Indeed public old-age pension provisions do not apply to, or at best stop far from guaranteeing subsistence levels for many who are in need of such assistance. Consequently the retiring employee *has* to rely on his company for the necessary support.

Actually companies in Japan had initiated old-age provisions for their employees long before any such efforts were undertaken in any respectable scale at the national level : contrary to the practice of West European nations (where the national governments took the lead in creating social security for the aged), in Japan it was the 'company family' which showed the way for later government prog- rammes to follow.

Severance and retirement pay are laid down in the rules of emp- loyment or in some special agreement with the company union. Involuntary separation (except for disciplinary cause) is always accompanied by much higher allowances than voluntary termina- tion. In the latter case in many firms, an employee is not entitled to any benefit unless he served the company for at least three years. For involuntary separation (excepting most cases of disciplinary dismissal), the employee is entitled to receive a lump sum after a shorter period of service (but still often not less than two years).

The amount of money to be paid is usually renegotiated between union and management every two or three years, or recently even more often. To determine the exact amount the last basic salary (on the date of retirement) is normally multiplied by somewhat less than the number of years worked in the firm, after which some modifica- tions can be added (related to the job classification, special merit, and so on). Since Japanese pay scales are still heavily characterized by a straightforward relation between age/seniority and earnings, after many years of service the retirement lump sum will amount to quite a substantial sum of money. For example, in 1975 the Ministry of Labour found in a sample of about 6000 companies with 30 or more regular employees that for retirement (for company reasons) the following average lump sum payments were made.

	Production workers (junior high school) (× 10,000 yen)	Non-production (senior high school) (× 10,000 yen)	Non-production (college, university) (× 10,000 yen)
after 5 years of service	22 (2.6 months)	28 (2.9 months)	32 (2.8 months)
after 10 years	60 (5.7 months)	73 (5.9 months)	92 (6.2 months)
after 20 years	197 (14.1 months)	244 (14.8 months)	299 (15.0 months)
after 30 years	380 (22.7 months)	477 (23.7 months)	619 (25.2 months)
after 35 years	474 (26.2 months)	600 (27.4 months)	—
after 40 years	568 (29.1 months)	—	—

Source: *Yearbook of Labour Statistics, 1975* (Tokyo: Ministry of Labour, 1976), p. 192-4. The data concern male employees only.

Company size plays a highly significant role when it comes to the amount the retiring employee is to receive. For example, a production worker with 40 years of service received in 1975 over 9.2 million yen (43.1 months' pay equivalent) in companies with 300-999 employees; over 6 million yen (31.6 months equivalent) in companies with 100-299 employees and almost 5.4 million yen (27.5 months) in companies with 30-99 employees. While over 90 per cent of companies sampled by the ministry (1975) had some kind of retirement allowance system in operation, almost 70 per cent of these just paid a one-time lump sum at once; about 13 per cent applied some sort of pension system, while almost 20 per cent (more than half of firms with 1,000 or more employees) combined a pension with a lump sum payment.

Pension plans have spread rapidly and became increasingly popular among employees. In 1962 a new law enabled companies with at least 20 employees to deduct 100 per cent of the employer's contributions to 'qualified pension plans' as business expenses. In March 1975, more than 94 per cent of the numerous qualified pension plans were non-contributory, i.e. employees did not contribute directly to them (notably in smaller firms). Only a small percentage of all companies pay a lifetime pension, while the rest pay a pension to former employees only during a certain fixed period, usually 10 years or at most 15. Eligibility for employees to participate in a pension scheme varies from firm to firm but the majority holds 10 years (90 per cent) or even 20 years to be the minimum period of seniority required for qualification. Directors, part-timers and temporary employees are mostly excluded; in over 45 per cent of companies sampled in 1975 participants could not receive benefits before 55 while an additional 42.6 per cent put the starting age at 60.

Japanese companies are increasingly concerned about the burden put on their shoulders both by the still largely seniority-based pay scales (which promise to lead towards even more gigantic disbursements in the future) and the ever-growing proportion of elderly employees (by 1980 more than half of the country's labour force will be at least 40 years of age; workers of 55 or older amounted to about 19 per cent of all employees in manufacturing industries in 1973 but are expected to amount to 28 per cent by 1985). The government is urged to help by establishing a viable national old age pension scheme and for their part companies are considering steps to reduce the significance of seniority in their pay-scale.

After retirement, management does not have any formal obligations to its former employees, though many companies these days are offering extended employment opportunities to some of their older personnel, raising the age limit effectively from 55 to 58 or even 60.

In larger firms it is rare to extend employment over the age of 60 (with the exception of the highest managerial levels), while this frequently is the case in smaller companies. However, such an extension of employment will mostly go along with a reduction in earnings and certainly the elimination of all automatic seniority-related pay increases, if still practised. (Actually, there is a trend in recent years to eliminate such automatic seniority-related increases from age 50 or even 45; after that age only performance-related increases and/or cost-of-living compensation applies; smaller companies have been forced to apply such systems for some time already, but recently even bigger firms have followed suit.) So even if the retirement age is extended from age 55 to 58 or higher, it is not unusual for the employee to be confronted with a steady or even abrupt drop in earnings.

What with public old-age pension provisions being grossly insufficient (cf. appendix 1 in this book) and retirement lump-sums (however impressive in their own right) not being enough to support one's life in retirement and that of one's dependants, it is no wonder that 80 per cent of Japan's elderly try to find new jobs after having had to leave the security of lifetime employment.

The retiring employee in Japan faces basically the same traumatic experiences as any other individual about to retire wherever his country or whatever his job. But for many Japanese there are additional snags: the company has become the primary base of life, even before his family. Employment for life with the same firm induces intense feelings of mutual attachment which by far surpass any other emotional ties. The retired Japanese therefore, is separated from the main vein of his existence at a relatively early age. His financial situation forces him to seek complementary employment and to build up new social relations at an age when most human beings prefer to quietly settle down. His position is not an easy one.

1. Takezawa S. *Changing worker values and their policy implications in Japan.* Mimeographed, New York, 1972. Also published in: Davis L. E. and Cherns A. B. eds *The quality of working life, volume I* (New York: Free Press, 1975).

2. Arai, S. *An intersection of east and west* (Tokyo: Rikugei, 1971), p. 128-9.

3. *Katsuyo rodo tokei 1977 (Compendium of labor statistics)* (Tokyo: Japan Productivity Center, 1977), p. 52; also Table 9 in Chapter 9 of this book. Note that after the wage gap had progressively narrowed down in previous years, in 1976 this trend was reversed, with older workers getting relatively higher wage raises than their younger colleagues.

4. For a clear example, see *Jokenbetsu chingin tokei* (Tokyo: Chamber of Commerce, 1971), p. 35.

5. Contrary to the prevailing situation elsewhere, the relatively high unemployment figures in Japan, after the oil crisis of 1973-74, did not so much concern the younger as well as the older layers of the total labour force.

Industry and formal education 5

Where lifetime employment is the prevailing practice management naturally will be inclined to skim the whole labour market in search of the cream of available manpower: those who will be granted entrance in the company as regular employees are supposed to stay there for their whole working career and management will not be able to dismiss them easily. Smaller firms are unable to offer working conditions comparable to those of large firms and it is inevitable that second-rate candidates will be the only ones available for them.

The first choice of annual manpower supply can be made from those who have just left school (or are about to do so), be it junior or senior high school, college or university.[1] The reasoning is that young people are inexpensive, easily indoctrinated and highly flexible to adapt to technological innovations, so those who will be offered lifetime employment and related privileges, will be preferably picked from this yearly fresh group. They are also the ones likely to be given the opportunity to gain membership of the core group of employees whose status is superior in the company's organization.

A basic distinction is to be made between recruitment practices for school leavers and practices for those who are recruited any other way. In this connection the question arises to which extent the Japanese system of formal education prepares its pupils for industrial employment.

Formal education versus vocational training

In Japan, even more than in many other countries, formal education is considered superior to vocational training. Traditionally, the relatively frequent inter-generation mobility from blue-collar family to the white-collar stratum through education channels has developed the notion of 'upward mobility through education'[2] which is often said to have made great advances in Japan.

Japanese institutions of formal education enjoy a preferential status as sources for labour recruitment as compared with a minor role for institutions of vocational training. Formal education starts with six years of elementary school followed by three years of junior high school (both compulsory). Junior high schools provide instruction in general subjects including Japanese language, social

studies, mathematics, science, music, fine arts and physical education. In addition, the teaching should include vocational training
covering such subjects as industry, commerce and fishery, taking
into consideration local conditions. In 1974 90 per cent of junior
high school leavers proceeded to further education while in turn
about one third of all senior high school leavers went on to universities (or similar). Senior high schools extend education for another
three years. They fall into one of three categories: those providing
only a *general* secondary course, those of a *comprehensive* type
with both a *general* course and specialized vocational courses, and
specialized vocational schools offering courses in one or more
fields of training. Many senior high schools offer just one vocational
course, instead of a choice of several alternatives, then being called
technical high schools or *commercial* high schools. By far the
greatest proportion of pupils follow the general education course.
When compared with the courses given at specific institutes for
vocational training, the vocational education offered at junior and
senior high schools is intended to impart to students social and
economic knowledge bearing on their future occupation: half the
time will be occupied by general subjects and the other half by
theoretical subjects in the specialized field of education. Courses at
vocational training institutes put more emphasis on applied practice and specific skills.

Japan's schools can stand comparison with those of any other
advanced nation, but the emphasis seems to be very much upon
memorizing with a concomitant neglect for independent insight
and logical reasoning. Entrance examinations generally carry decisive significance for many young Japanese. It may sound unbelievable, but the choice of the right kindergarten is regarded by quite a
few parents as the first important step to an attractive career during
adulthood. If not at kindergarten the 'ladder of success' or 'social
chimney' in many cases is supposed to begin with the choice of an
elementary school. The chain of entrance examinations extends
from 'prestigious' elementary schools, junior and senior high
schools (supposedly having good records of placing their pupils at
'good' universities) to college or university, each phase requiring
careful tactics, mainly on the part of the mothers. (It may be
emphasized here that the role of the father in the typical Japanese
family, particularly in the education of the male children, tends to be
minor, that of the mother being decisive indeed.) All this holds
particularly true for those who want to pass through the best universities about which one frequently hears comments like: '. . . the only
problem is how to get in; once you are there, you may be sure of
your future career, even if you do not do a thing!'. Even though the
initial selection process is strict, the familiar character of Japanese
social groups operates in the university setting: 'to treat all students

leniently and sometimes indulgently once they are admitted'.[3] Entrance examinations do tend to be very stiff. Parents spend large amounts of money for extra lessons or special preparatory schools. With just cause, the Japanese speak of the 'examination hell' which each year leaves suicides in its wake.

Only the very brilliant and self-confident child of a poor family may be able to pass the entrance examination into a bright future, while the majority of students at the best national universities come from a relatively rich background. In addition, studying at private universities is more expensive which in fact creates a barrier for the realization of the often so highly praised social mobility and equal chances available to everyone in Japan. The State gives national universities virtually 100 per cent financial support but only 17 or 18 per cent of their operating cost to most private universities that have to bear the brunt of higher education. Most of them are near the brink of their long-sustained financial crisis and this is clearly reflected in the quality of their education. General-subjects lectures are given in packed classrooms by inadequately paid lecturers while many students make it quite clear that to them the university is simply a means of finding a job, a mere step towards personal success. A well-known Japanese professor once referred to his own university as a kindergarten and it is not an exaggeration to say that social activities often seem at least as important as more scholarly or academic ones.

Industry's criteria

Industry does not seem to mind. Technological innovations take place with such speed that the recent graduate's technical knowledge will soon be obsolete anyway. According to the personnel manager of a very large firm '. . . we can teach them everything once they are with us. I do not like men with a highly specialized knowledge of one field or another: they think they know everything and you cannot do a thing with them. We prefer to get a blank page where the company can freely write down what it thinks desirable. Schools should give us the right kind of men: not the brainy kind who know everything about some small thing but the fellow who can get along with others in the company and is open to new knowledge, the flexible man.' From this point of view it looks like industry is not necessarily very unhappy about the deplorable conditions under which the majority of university students are educated. Industry has taken to training and educating its own personnel according to its own needs.

In pre-war days large companies used to entertain special ties with a limited number of high-prestige universities. For their part universities would do their utmost to preserve the profitable rela-

58

tions with major enterprises. The position is still largely the same today, with large companies drawing fresh manpower from the better universities: the lower the position of the company the lower the probable ranking of the universities from which most graduates are recruited for employment.

A crucial figure in the recruitment procedure is the *sensei:* a professor or teacher. There often exist close personal ties between some students and one particular *sensei,* very much like the European paternal relationship. For each student only one *sensei* can take this place, resulting in a wide variety of lifetime obligations. The *sensei* therefore plays an essential role for the job-seeking student. At the very least he will write a letter of recommendation, or he may use the better of his influence to arrange an offer from a desirable enterprise, contacting his former students or company officials with whom he has special relations. Many firms employ 'contact-persons' whose main activities consist of keeping in touch with particular universities, through professors or other influential officials.

In every major company one encounters informal groups of graduates from the same university: they have a very substantial impact upon the total organization even though their network of interpersonal ties is barely reflected in the formal organization chart of the company, if at all. Intense feelings of rivalry and competition may characterize the relations between several such university cliques. An acquaintance of mine who was offered a job by a well-known firm in spite of his poor performance during selection procedures was later told repeatedly that he had been hired mainly because of the fact that his university's group in the company had been weakened after some years during which the personnel department had been dominated by a rival university clique. According to Chie Nakane '. . . education creates more effective relationships than kinship . . . a common educational background comes next to institution or place of work in degree of function and is more effective than either family or local background'.[4]

Screening

Every year voluminous directories with a variety of information about numerous companies are made available to prospective applicants, usually through the school's employment information office. They take the place of advertisements in the papers. The large majority of university graduates hoping to be employed in major firms undergoes a thorough screening by private detectives, mostly without the applicants' knowledge.

The recruitment of those who leave either junior or senior high school basically follows the same lines as described for university graduates. Those who have finished junior high school (at about 14) are destined to fill blue-collar production jobs. Their screening is often restricted to some police information or a recommendation by a senior employee. High school leavers may be recruited from specific districts only : the common regional background provides a dependable basis for closer personal relations and for several influential but informal groups. Several large firms report recruiting only school leavers from *senior* high school, no *junior* high school leavers at all ; this is said to be done in order not to deprive smaller firms of their share of unskilled labour, but at least one more consideration must be that internal training programmes can be attuned to the higher level of previous education, making extensive courses of general knowledge unnecessary.

In line with the Employment Measures Law of 1966 an intricate network of *Public Employment Security Offices* (PESO) has been set up, using a computerized data processing system, to 'enable workers to find jobs suitable to their abilities and enabling enterprises to obtain men of talent'.[5] A large number of men and women aged between 20 and 24 utilize the services of PESO, which may be explained with reference to the relatively high mobility in the earliest years of employment.[6]

Even though outside *recruitment agencies* have now existed for quite some time they still seem to operate largely in the margin. Foreign firms are more inclined to apply for their help, Japanese management apparently having to overcome some aversion before resorting to their assistance.

1. In Chapter 7 it will be pointed out that institutes of vocational training can scarcely compare to educational institutes as sources of new, young manpower.

2. Hideaki Okamoto. *Vocational training in Japan* (Tokyo : Japan Institute of Labour, 1969), 6-10.

3. Michio Nagai. *Higher education in Japan : its take-off and crash* Dusenbury J. transl. (Tokyo : University of Tokyo Press, 1971), p. 86. Mr Nagai was Minister of Education in the Miki cabinet, 1974-1976, too short a time to bring about real change even though he tried hard to get things moving.

4. Chie Nakane. *Japanese society* (London : Weidenfeld and Nicolson, 1970), p. 128.

5. *Labour administration in Japan, 1971* (Tokyo : Ministry of Labour, 1971), 13-5. The advanced on-line system used has drawn admiring reports from experts all over the world as an exceptional technological achievement.

6. Because unemployment hit particularly hard at higher age brackets in the recession following the 1973-74 oil crisis, recent years have seen growing proportions (it was said) of middle-aged and older hopefuls approaching the PESO's.

The process of selection   6

Candidates for regular employee status are subjected to a series of checks in order to investigate the probability of their becoming desirable members of the stable manpower reservoir in the large firm. Smaller companies follow much simpler methods to select new personnel. In major enterprises more attention is paid to those who are likely to be future employees in important administrative, technical or managerial areas than to prospective blue-collar production workers. It should be noted that most selection activities are practised only for those who might be granted regular employee status. The usual selection procedures are not so much geared towards judging a specific kind of aptitude, skill or proficiency but rather towards finding out personality traits as the ability to associate and get along with others, learning potential and conformism.

'Desirable personality'

The selection *interview* probably is the most common and widespread tool for selection of new personnel, both in big and small firms. Some firms arrange for two or more interviews to take place, particularly for university graduates. Interviews may occasionally take the form of group discussions, with some company officials and one or more applicants. Whatever its form, invariably the main intention of the selection interview is to obtain an impression of the applicant's personality. Keeping in mind how important a smooth functioning of 'the group' is considered to be in Japan and also that ideally an employee is to be hired for life, one will understand the vital necessity to make sure that any new employee has the 'desirable personality'. Therefore a great flexibility and a sharp sense of preserving harmonious group relations will be the main criteria and the 'blank page' type of candidate will be preferred. Graduation from one of the better universities or high schools and/or proper *introductions* serve as a sort of guarantee for the applicant's personality. School reports may be studied to determine the general level of intelligence and industriousness, while family background is also considered.

Written entrance examinations are the rule in the great majority of (especially larger) firms. The higher the level of educational attainment before recruitment, the more weight may be given to the results of the examination. Yet those who come from a 'better' university do not have to worry too much about the outcome : they will be hired anyway. But for the applicant who is a graduate of a lesser university the results may be of decisive influence, along with the impression made during the interviews and the quality of his personal references. For him the company entrance examinations, of which he takes on average three, loom ahead long before they are taken, while the choice of companies where to try one's luck is a matter of intensive discussion with friends, relations and professors.

For social-science graduates (the majority at Japanese universities) the examination usually consists of an essay on some relevant topic but unquestionably the interview remains of most importance for this category. In the case of a technical-science graduate more attention will be paid to the results of his written examination. In fact, if not intentionally, his entrance examination tends to test mainly the ability to reproduce memorized facts and figures and not so much variables as insight or initiative, much less specialized knowledge. Where Japanese management (unlike its American counterpart) cannot easily fire personnel, selection seems to focus rather on conformity (somehow tapped in interviews and written examination, as well as school reports) than on highly individualistic characteristics or outstanding abilities.

It has been said that it does not make much sense in Japan to use any of the known *psychological tests :* once a Japanese is taken out of his group environment, he will behave and react completely differently from the way he would under normal circumstances. Whatever the truth, psychological testing certainly does not take place on a large scale. Testing of vocational interests is held to be rather superfluous insofar as through lifetime employment the individual is supposed to gradually find his optimum scope and satisfaction through company training and numerous transfers. Psychological testing does not really seem to fit in the Japanese employment practice. One manager put it this way : 'We have an old saying "protruding nails will be hammered down" and if we would use tests to clearly reveal differences among our people we would act in the opposite way ; that is why most tests used in industry are made to serve the traditional purpose—to make sure that the applicant will fit in the total employee group, nothing more. The time is past when we had to introduce everything western on the assumption that it was superior to Japanese ways ; what has been introduced has been altered to fit into our traditional pattern and that is what happened to psychological tests as well.'

In view of lifetime employment one would expect virtually all applicants for employment in modern Japan to be subjected to a *physical examination* but this is not such a general practice as one might anticipate. There is a clear relation between company size and the occurrence of physical check-up: the larger the firm, the more likely it is for such an examination to be mandatory. Virtually everywhere, however, some kind of official health certificate is normally requested as part of the standard selection procedure.

A wide variety of other selection tools might be listed. Most firms require some kind of *personal history* (for which standard forms can be bought at any stationery shop). *School reports* are asked in the case of younger applicants and in addition *police information* may be requested. *Family background* often is investigated and if an applicant has had *previous work* experience, some declaration may be required from his former employer.

Once more: selection in Japanese industry tries to concentrate heavily upon 'desirable personality', with a relative neglect for specific aptitudes and abilities. This is particularly true in the case of recent school leavers (or graduates-to-be) who are regarded as potentially regular employees.

Mutual commitment

In present-day Japan *individual labour contracts* normally are used only in the case of temporary or part-time employment. Such contracts do not exceed the legal limit of one year. In bigger enterprises a newly selected employee, after the probation period, may be requested to sign a document—*seiyakusho*—which then takes the place of an individual labour contract and exists along with the collective labour agreement. One could consider this procedure as a ceremony in which the new employee gives a formal pledge of commitment to the company by pressing his seal on the document. This is not a real contract, and the company does not endorse it either but in accepting the pledge of loyalty, management implicitly commits itself to guarantee the employee's job security for the rest of his working career. In other words, mutual lifetime-employment commitment as such is nowhere explicitly mentioned in individual or collective labour agreements or in employment regulations. The signing of a seiyakusho by a new regular employee is merely an expression of the intention to remain loyal to the company and to perform dutifully whatever tasks may be required. The company is *implicitly* understood to play the complementary role without anything like it being formally stated.

Initial job assignments and task descriptions

Seldom are any detailed descriptions given about duties to be performed (in spite of a recent trend to the opposite, this still can be maintained). Rather one will find a delineation of the place where the employee is supposed to work: his *shokuba*. *Shokuba* means literally work place but includes a wide range of social and emotional connotations: it is going to be the direct group environment upon which the employee will largely depend for the further development of his abilities. In many cases of transfer an employee receives a new 'task description', a document which again keeps virtually silent about the duties to be performed but instead mentions the new place of work and maybe the name of the group leader or superior to whom he is assigned. On the other hand it is quite normal for work *groups* to be given a concrete task description. Each division may make up a rough outline, delineating the activities of every section in general terms. The description tends to become more detailed as one goes down the line, specially at the workgroup level where it stops. A sort of intuitive consensus within the group results in an understanding of work division to which the most responsible group member is supposed to give explicit expression. In other words this is *group responsibility* rather than individual responsibility, and in this pattern detailed individual task descriptions just do not fit too well.[1] This also implies, in fact, that, as a unit, the Japanese work group is autonomous to quite an extent. Employees may be required to perform a wide variety of duties which may or may not be in line with their previous education or training.

Individual job assignments also fit into this picture: the first job given to any new employee is very simple and—more often than not—has barely any relation to his previous schooling. Even though the treatment of three employees with junior, senior high school and university background will differ greatly in the long term, initially it may be quite similar. University graduates frequently work at the production level for some time in order to get acquainted with the company's main products; this is in accordance with 'the strong belief among (Japanese) management that education within the company is better than formal education outside'.[2] Creating a flexible manpower force with *strong adaptability* is one of the primary aims.

Indoctrination

All large firms provide a special programme of initial training and education for their new employees: this is not confined to vocational training but covers a broad 'cultural' range. The introduction programme is normally shorter for blue-collar than for white-collar personnel. In many a company brochure such programmes are openly referred to as 'indoctrination courses', intended to foster total commitment to the organization. Since the total structure of Japanese society and education seems to be geared towards the denial of selfish individualist tendencies, most Japanese will fit relatively easily into this pattern but whoever refuses to submit to such presuppositions is automatically at a disadvantage. Those who have too much foreign experience are utterly suspect: the probability of having picked up selfish inclinations is considered to be enormous. If only the company's interest becomes one of the employee's primary concerns, the company will respond to this total commitment generously through lifetime job security and ample fringe benefits.

Newcomers may be trained at *out-of-company gatherings* for some days and on repeated occasions during their first year or so, sometimes in a mountain lodge, a hot spring resort hotel or a seaside villa, many of these retreats being company property. Group gatherings such as these are regarded as valuable because they create a strong group cohesiveness among the newcomers of each year. On the other hand participants at these early meetings are closely observed in order to identify potential candidates for special treatment in the future (the participants mostly being aware of this observation, so that a fairly typical combination of 'fostering group cohesion' simultaneously with 'stimulating interpersonal competition' is brought about). In addition, *in-company introduction courses* are quite common for all categories of new employees.

Whatever the location or duration of these courses, the most common activities emphasize motivation and the right company spirit.

At least as important as group introduction are *individual guidance programmes* within the company, often conducted by slightly senior employees ('older brother' or 'older sister'): employees who have worked hard and shown no undesirable propensities for three or four years after employment are asked to take charge of two or three newcomers. This tends to create a sense of confidence in the newcomers since the age difference is small. The results are even better if the older brother (or senior colleague) and the newcomers are from the same province: he will be even more eager to give advice not only regarding work but also on matters regarding private life. Not only are the older brothers and sisters supposed to provide assistance to newcomers, in many cases they are also intended to be an important source of information about the new employees' personality, convictions and behaviour. For this purpose, regular meetings are held with supervisors and personnel officials. The Japanese superior not only concerns himself with production and results, but also tries to make himself familiar with more personal circumstances of his subordinates.

Most larger and many smaller firms operate *dormitories* for their bachelor workers. The head of the dormitory, who serves as the employer's direct representative, gives information and assistance to the inmates while also reporting about them to the company. In spite of certain stipulations in the Labour Standards Law, many dormitory rules seem highly restrictive on the individual inhabitants, e.g. entitling the head to enter any room for inspection at any time. Trainees' dormitories seem to offer harshest conditions, but rather severe limitations on individual rights are commonplace almost anywhere. This in addition to often cramped quarters. Yet, while companies appear to appreciate the possibility of keeping a close watch upon their newest manpower acquisition through the dormitory, recent graduates may gladly sacrifice part of their privacy in order to get at least some housing, at low prices for that matter.

In this context a typical Japanese practice can be mentioned: many firms hold some kind of *morning ceremony*—a five-minute talk, the company song or even some physical exercises performed to a rigid pattern—whose main purpose is to strengthen identification and loyalty.

It is quite common that aspiring employees have to pass a *probationary period,* varying in length from one to six months. Many firms think it necessary to impose extra checks on workers with previous employment experiences elsewhere. During the probationary period, a new employee is treated as a temporary worker, and therefore is not considered eligible for membership in the company union.

After his probation, the newcomer may be promoted to the category of regular employee if he has proved to be receptive to the 'company culture'. Statistics show a relatively high turnover rate during the earlier years of employment after leaving school: apparently many youngsters have trouble subduing their wishes to the company requirements.

While this seems to be the case in other industrialized societies as well, the 'indoctrination' pressure seems to be much greater in Japan (some even speak of 'brainwashing Japanese style').

The great majority of Japanese are not used to asserting their individuality: for most, the transition from school life into company life will be relatively easy and the firm rewards the faithful with a 'warm atmosphere' and relatively generous payments. Contrastingly, resistance against the 'company culture' offers no viable alternative: at best one may be tolerated in the big firm (but without favourable career prospects) or one has to leave the better firms and be submerged into the lower layers of Japan's dual structure (where, perhaps, the individual is given a slightly better chance, but financial and other conditions are far inferior). For many this bleak alternative must be sufficient reason for gradual resignation.[3] The typical 'sarari-man' may be the best illustration of this phenomenon: relatively happy, quite dedicated but definitely colourless.

1.   Several authors refer to this collective responsibility. To name a few only: Chie Nakane *Japanese society* (London: Weidenfeld and Nicolson, 1970), 80-6; Johnson R. T. and Ouchi W. G. Made in America (under Japanese management). *Harvard Bus. Rev.*, Sept.-Oct. 1974, 61-9; Whitehill A. and Takezawa S. *The other worker—a comparative study of industrial relations in the United States and Japan* (Honolulu: East-West Center Press, 1968), 286-9; Arai S. *An intersection of East and West* (Tokyo: Rikugei, 1971), 147-8. See also my *Blue-collar workers in Japan and Holland: a comparative study* (Meppel-Holland, 1977).

2.   *Japan Labour Bull.,* Sept 1, 1971.

3.   This was one of the more obvious findings in my own study (as reported in *Blue-collar workers in Japan and Holland):* '. . . in Japan rising age goes together with increased 'social capital', satisfaction and identification with the company, whereas in Holland dissatisfaction seems to increase with rising age, workers tend more to fence themselves off from management and instead to identify with the peer group.' (p. 238).

Training   7

The first decades of Japan's industrialization were characterized mainly by the 'seeing and doing' type of training such as had been usual before 1870. During those early years skilled workers tended to pursue the highest rewards, which resulted in very high mobility rates among skilled labour. There were virtually no craft unions of skilled workers operating their own system of apprenticeship training.

Before long, larger companies took the prerogative of skill training into their own hands, while offering lifetime employment security and other privileges to skilled workers in order to bind them to the firm as instructors for unskilled personnel. This was the beginning of lifetime employment guarantees for blue-collar workers in Japan's industry.

Another factor which lay at the root of permanent employment for a key group of blue-collar workers and of company-initiated training programmes was the fact that big enterprises introduced their new technology from all over the western world (mainly Great Britain, USA and Germany, and to a lesser extent from France and Italy). Machines, tools and all other necessary equipment which were introduced from each of these countries varied greatly in design and operation. Since public vocational training at the time was very limited, each large company felt compelled to arrange for its own skill-training courses, in view of the specific machinery that had been installed in its plants. Therefore, skills tended to become inconvertible among companies : employees had to remain with the company where they had received their training.

Public vocational training

Public vocational training never really has played a crucial role within the Japanese labour-market process. In prewar days, technical high schools produced some numbers of technicians but failed to obtain a central position. Public vocational training in the strict sense was mainly given to the unemployed who wanted to grasp this chance for advancement in medium and smaller size enterprises.

After the war much was done to improve both quantity and quality of public vocational courses, be it with only limited success. Vocational training once more came to be established in the offices for vocational guidance and development, which were set up as devices to fight unemployment.

Table 5

SYSTEM OF VOCATIONAL TRAINING

Kinds of Vocational Training	Training course	Training method	Training period
Basic training	General training	(1) Full-time	1 year
		(2) Full-time	1 year or 6 months
	Advanced training	(1) Full-time	3 years or 2 years
		(2) Full-time	2 years or 1 year
Upgrading training	Training for second grade certified skilled workers	Full-time	1 month
		Part-time	6 months
		Correspondence	1 year
	Supervisory training	Part-time (TWI*, PST† PDI‡ are conducted)	within 11 days
	Technician training	Full-time	1 year
Occupational capacity re-development training	Job conversion training	Full-time	within 1 year
		Part-time	within 1 year
Updating training	Additional skill training	Part-time	6 days per subject
	Supplementary skill training	Part-time	6 days per subject
Instructor training	Long term instructor-training	Full-time	4 years
	Short-term instructor-training	Full-time	6 months
	Instructor updating training	Full-time	1 month

Remarks:
(1) for junior high school graduates.
(2) for senior high school graduates.
*Training within industry †Problem-solving training ‡Programme Development Institute.

At present public vocational training is conducted under the responsibility of the central government, prefectural governments, city, town and village authorities and of the Employment Promotion Projects Corporation, and is mostly free of charge. Table 5 gives a comprehensive view of the kinds of vocational training, type of training courses, training methods and their duration.

Institutions where public vocational training is given can be described as follows: *general vocation training centres,* which provide mainly basic general training courses and retraining; *advanced vocational training centres* providing basic and advanced training courses and retraining; *vocational training centres for physically handicapped persons* and *the Institute of Vocational Training* which provides instructor training and conducts studies regarding vocational training. The training standards for all public vocational training courses are provided in a Ministerial Ordinance of the Ministry of Labour. In spite of the numerous efforts to improve the image of public vocational training, the clearly preferred channel of career development for a Japanese youth is not through public but through intracompany training, to be started upon leaving school, college or university.

Authorized vocational training

An important part of public vocational training is carried out at authorized training facilities of enterprises or groups of enterprises designated by the prefectural governors: in this way a formal link is created between public and in-plant training schedules through which firms accept minimum standards set by the Ministry of Labour. Government helps by providing instructors, text books and sometimes financial support.

There seems to exist a strong preference among those who have successfully taken a course for vocational-training instructors to work for authorized training centres (i.e. for private industry) rather than for public vocational institutes.

Authorized vocational training centres whether based at a single company or operated jointly by several co-operating firms may be either 'general' or 'advanced' and therefore offer similar courses under at least the same standards and conditions as the public facilities. In 1972 there were about 126,500 persons who successfully completed courses at any of the public vocational training centres, and in 1971 the total number of trainees at authorized training facilities did not reach 100,000. One may safely conclude that only a very limited proportion of the employed population in Japan follows any public vocational training at all.[1] Okamoto confirms this when he writes about in-plant vocational training that the number of trainees 'mean only a very small portion of a great number of workers and enterprises in medium and small sectors in Japan. Many are developing their occupational capacity and personalities under the unstructured apprenticeship of artisans and foremen or merely through intuition and knack . . .'[2]

Standards

In major enterprises, however, the standards maintained for vocational training curricula (authorized or not) are usually much higher than those which have been set by the Ministry of Labour.

Both practical, theoretical and general training and education at major enterprises are of undeniably high quality. Because of this high level, numerous large firms do not care much about the official public training facilities, neither do they really bother to foster any important links with the public system of vocational training. The latter system is thus reduced to no more than the second plan, at best, while major private enterprises actually carry the lion's share in the vocational training of Japan's working population.

On-the-job training

Both among merchants and craftsmen of Japan's traditional society, training was largely conducted through a system of apprenticeships, in which on-the-job training with clearly defined stages of learning was the most outstanding feature. At present, such apprenticeship patterns play an important role in the training of workers in numerous small manufacturing workshops, which together make up a significant part of the lower layers of Japan's dual economic structure. On-the-job training, whether or not performed through informal apprenticeship relations, has been and still is one of the main sources of Japanese skilled manpower.

The pre-war system of workman apprenticeships proved to have serious limitations: it was too much geared towards instruction of manual skills, without a commensurate concern for a technical understanding of the skills acquired. Consequently, such skills tended to be less adaptive to technological change. In economic terms, the system was unable to keep up with the demand for newer skills. The trainee tended to become a rather one-sided person, not a flexible employee ready to meet changes.

Over the years there have been distinct efforts to supplement or even replace the apprenticeship system, particularly in larger enterprises, even though here also on-the-job training has remained the outstanding pivot of company training. In smaller firms, learning through 'seeing and doing' along with 'intuition and knack' have remained the rule to the present day.

'In Europe, education tends to impart knowledge and skills to individuals to prepare them for expertise in a rather specialized field. In Japan, the scope tends to be broader. If a man is willing and capable he should be allowed to learn. The Japanese tend to be rather egalitarian in their thoughts about individual abilities: most people have the necessary abilities to perform a great many jobs. Japanese do not like the fact of previous education limiting future possibilities: give people the job and they will learn!'[3]

After a period of basic training, followed by virtually all new employees of major firms, an extensive series of job transfers and various work assignments take place. Japanese managers try to find out about their subordinates' strong points, weak points, personality, etc, so that among senior managers a collective consensus will grow about the potential of junior managers. Gradually many employees will end up where they fit best, not only as far as their abilities but also as far as interpersonal relations are concerned.

Company training centres

Whether or not officially recognized as Authorized Training Facilities, vocational training courses are provided at company training centres of most major firms. This training is given as a preparation for national trade-skill tests or for the sake of transfer training. Skill certificates are, by law, necessary for performing certain types of work, for example the handling of specific kinds of electrical equipment. Transfer training is usually given as economic circumstances cause management to reduce recruitment and to arrange adaptation training for specific groups of workers, including older ones. In addition, a typical company training centre provides a whole gamut of courses aimed at improving practical skills, related technical knowledge and more general subjects. (In 1955 training centres were operated in only about 20 per cent of the largest firms—of 5,000 employees or more—but by 1970 a company centre was available in about 80 per cent of similar firms.)

The instructors are a mixture of the firms own experts, experts from other firms with which the company has particular ties, experts from outside training institutes and university professors. About one-third of textbooks in use at the training centres is developed and readjusted by the company's staff.

Selection criteria

On the whole it is management and not so much the man's own inclinations which decides the career pattern of individual workers; the major criterion brought to this selection process revolves around the worker's *general behaviour* and *personality* rather than his specific job performance or skills. 'Behaviour' as such, of course, is not necessarily commensurate with highest ability or quality of job performance but rather, it usually implies proven dedication and desirable personality characteristics. In addition, since the training system heavily relies upon on-the-job training and job experience, management possesses through work assignments and successive transfers a potent means to give special training chances to selected individuals.

At blue-collar level, on-the-job training is entrusted to the supervisor, the foreman or a senior colleague (core-group members):

that is why training and education of supervisors receive great emphasis in Japanese industry. In addition to technical subjects an important aspect of supervisory training is 'how to train'. On-the-job training may be supplemented with carefully planned off-the-job courses which are usually given at the company training centre.

Generally white-collar and managerial training schedules are less formalized, with a heavier emphasis upon learning through successive work assignments and regular transfers. Training is systematized to a higher extent for white-collar employees with just senior high-school background than for those who graduated from college or university. It is a rare senior high-school leaver who succeeds in keeping up with those who completed college or university education.

Training and education of higher management

Like in the blue-collar stratum, training tends to be more specifically subject-oriented in the earlier phases of a university graduate's career, while later on more stress will be put upon general or cultural subjects, character-building and other related concepts. Whoever fails to pass the examinations of lower-level courses, is not admitted to the next course and therefore suffers a serious setback for future career chances. Actually this often means no more than seniority-based promotion.

Graduates from institutes of high education are in their majority to be trained to become section chief at around the age of 40 and for this purpose they follow a variety of courses within or without the company, the specific subject matter being decided as need dictates. They reach the position of section chief easily and almost automatically. For most of them, their formal training tends to diminish by the time they approach this point.

Higher ranks in the hierarchy are to be occupied only by those who have participated in a substantial number of extra courses and have demonstrated their superior ability.

Within the total group of university graduates a ready means of differentiation is to be found in the speed with which an employee is introduced into a variety of subjects areas through various assignments and transfers, and in the tempo of his successive admissions to courses. Almost all university graduates will become section chief in due course, but a small number of them will reach this position well in advance of the others and these are the ones to be considered as the likely candidates for higher managerial positions in the not too distant future. Their training is also likely to be effected through regular lectures, problem-solving sessions and yearly seminars on specific fashionable subjects. Top management occasionally participates in similar programmes.

Studying outside the company

Large companies annually send a number of white-collar employees to outside training institutes or universities, both in Japan
and in foreign countries. The company pays all expenses and, contrary to individuals who went to study abroad on their own initiative,
those who follow courses with the backing of their firm can be quite
sure of greatly improved career chances after their return from
abroad. The preparation of employees who are going to be sent
abroad is intensive and covers language training to table manners.
Duty abroad is often regarded as one of the necessary high-level job
transfers which prepare a manager for important positions in the
years to come. The same may be said about the exchange of personnel with government agencies such as the Ministry of International Trade and Industry, the Economic Planning Agency and the
Finance Ministry. The company's future leaders can thus get
acquainted personally with those government officials and institutions that they will have to deal with later on, at the same time
obtaining a thorough familiarity with the most successful procedures and channels in the governmental area concerned.

Outside training institutes

Before concluding this chapter some reference must be made to the
numerous outside training institutes which operate on a private or
semi-official basis. A cautious estimate (by a Japanese expert) indicates that there are more than 500 such institutes in the Tokyo-
Kanagawa area alone (1977).

Generally speaking, these organizations dispatch their experts to
member and client companies to assist management in its training
activities and provide advice; they also organize their own courses
to which companies can send participants.

Self-development

Employees of many companies are urged to work hard for 'self-
development'. Thousands of young people follow correspondence
courses with a great diversity of objectives.

'The term "self-development" has attained particular prominence
recently as we enter a period of ability-orientation in management. It
points up the personal effort required to develop one's individual
capabilities to the ultimate, where "capability" is understood to
refer not only to the knowledge, expertise and attitudes required for
work accomplishment, but to the broader aspects of personality as
well. This is because the higher one rises in the corporate pyramid,
the keener the need for self-development, and the greater the extent
to which capability concerns thinking which rises above directly
work-connected factors; that is, the development of a personality

which can gain the confidence of subordinates and become a focus of leadership.'[4]

In many cases this kind of 'self-development' has been pursued along with similar activities such as the self-appraisal system and 'management-by-objectives'. In other cases, employees are urged to make a good use of their leisure time, occasionally to such an extent that even very loyal company unions have to protest against infringement upon the employees' private lives.

Broadcasting

Japanese radio and television play a role of considerable importance in the spreading of knowledge and information among the total population. A well-known example is the series of teaching programmes on quality control in the 1950s and 1960s which accompanied the tremendous upsurge of quality-control movement in all Japanese industry. Most such programmes are intended to supplement regular school education and are dominated by the work of the Japan Broadcasting Corporation (NHK) which continues to develop very extensive educational programmes both on radio and television.[5]

1. The Ministry of Labour reaches the same conclusion: see *Vocational training in Japan* (Tokyo: Ministry of Labour, 1972), p. 40.

2. Okamoto H. *Vocational training in Japan* (Tokyo: Japan Institute of Labour, 1969), p. 11. One more typical point should be mentioned about public vocational training: the very heavy over-representation of trainees for the building industry.

3. This is an almost literal quote from a 1977 conversation with a Japanese manager in charge of training and education.

4. Nakayama S. The furthering of self-development. In *Reading on managing employees* (Tokyo: Asian Productivity Organization, 1971), 45-56.

5. For an authoritative analysis of educational broadcasting in Japan (up to the late 1960s), see M. Nishimoto: *The development of educational broadcasting in Japan* (Tokyo: Sophia University), 1969.

Hierarchy 8

Classification and promotion of personnel

If previous chapters have occasionally demonstrated some tension existing within Japanese industrial society because of conflicting elements in traditional patterns and new practices, the area of employee classification—with all its concomitants—seems to be right at the heart of this tension.

Traditional classification was built upon three essential elements: lifetime employment, level of previous educational attainment and length of service. To give a very rough description of this traditional system: whoever had been granted the privilege of lifetime employment security could be certain both about his remaining employed till retirement age or death and about seniority-based steady promotion and remuneration (according to the pattern for employees with the same kind of educational background). Those who failed to secure lifetime employment were also by and large excluded from seniority-based promotion and remuneration. Actual work performance and demonstrated ability barely counted as determinants for career progress. Consequently it was not unusual to meet a manager lacking substantial managerial ability who had been promoted only on the basis of seniority and even had been assigned subordinates without ever having received a clear definition of duties and responsibilities.

In recent decades considerable tensions have been building up around this traditional system. Here are some pointers: the greatly increased numbers of personnel with the privilege of lifetime employment security, combined with the labour shortage in the latter half of the 1960s, resulted in heightened levels of turnover, particularly among younger workers; management was confronted with pressure from its better educated manpower to improve promotion chances and to provide more worthwhile work; moreover, the sharp rises in starting salaries over the years resulted in a substantial relative devaluation of the remuneration for older employees who saw the youngsters eat away at their own long-term 'investments'. Meanwhile supervisors were burdened with considerably broadened job responsibilities, in relation to rapidly advancing technological requirements and rising employee expectations. The enormous technological developments even threatened to turn seniority into a liability: management sensed the necessity of a more efficient system of promotion in which seniority prerogatives might have to be largely disregarded and exceptional career progress might have to be offered to the most able candidates. In this connection expressions like 'job-centred approach' or 'ability management' were frequently used. It was clearly felt that strict continuation of the traditional system of classification could hardly be combined with modern and efficient management practices. On the other hand there seems to have been a widespread consensus that modernization efforts ought to be based upon 'Japanese ways', which meant that some form of seniority system ought to be preserved. (At present, this 'battle of views' is still being hotly discussed.)

Meanwhile, as a compromise between all these considerations, the so-called *shikaku seido* (qualification classification system) was developed and found widespread acceptance all over Japan. This system is a departure from the traditional 'status classification system' in that, in principle, employees are classified rather according to some 'qualifications', i.e. their supposedly available level of knowledge, proficiency, experience, skill and 'general capabilities', than on the basis of their sex, level of formal educational attainment and length of service (as used to be practised). Within this *shikaku seido* the work actually performed has only secondary importance: it is primarily the level of his potential contribution which determines an employee's place in the company hierarchy. Thus one may encounter a number of cases where a man performs work which is inferior (or barely related) to the official rank and title which he is allowed to carry.

Initial personnel classification

A new employee is classified into a sort of introductory category or into a very broad job category such as production, clerical or technical personnel. This is a fairly automatic process, mainly depending upon his previous education.

Every company has very clear rules concerning this *initial classification* of new employees. For example a rather old, big manufacturing company in the Tokyo area used the following standards (according to information obtained in 1972). School leavers from junior high school are not hired at all; school leavers from senior high school are put in grade 1 of the lowest job group of the production category, or of the so-called 'special' category (porter, security men, driver); graduates from four-year university are put in grade 1 of the second job group of the technical or the office category depending on the subject read; graduates from six-year university are put in grade 1 of the third job group of the technical or the office category, again depending on the subject read.

A large department store in Tokyo reports that all new entrants must pass a one-year probation period, after which senior high-school graduates will be placed in the first (lowest) grade of the lowest salesmen group, college graduates in the second grade of the same group and university graduates in the second grade of the second lowest salesmen group.

In the case of non-graduate recruitment, after a probationary test period a classification decision is made, based upon previous education, previous work experience, initial performance and perhaps examination results. (For a more detailed outline of career possibilities under shikaku seido see Appendix 2.)

Position hierarchy versus status hierarchy

Thus, for the sake of initial classification of new personnel, the traditional pattern is still closely followed: each of the three model-employee types (junior-, senior- high-school leavers or university graduates) is classified according to sex and previous educational attainment. Under the traditional system of personnel classification, promotion all through one's career tended to be pretty much the same for all members of each of the three model-employee types.

Through the *shikaku seido* management trusts to have developed a system of classification and promotion which allows, at the one hand, to utilize and reward excellent performance and capacity, while at the same time seniority rights and steady 'status' progress can be at least partially maintained as a stimulus for continued loyalty. Since only a minority of all employees in fact is lifted out because of their superior capacity or performance, these are the *core-group* members whose additional responsibility is rewarded with slightly higher pay and *in fact* more status. However, their less able colleagues, who do not get into the core-group, are still promoted steadily, often to carry titles which resemble the ones in the core-group. Two parallel hierarchies can thus be distinguished (at least by insiders): a *position hierarchy* (corresponding to actual duties and responsibilities), and a *status hierarchy* (corresponding to potential functioning, based upon mere qualifications). Both hierarchies frequently overlap, but where the system actually is in operation it is through the position hierarchy (core-group membership) that most real promotions are gained and the best future prospects can be acquired. It must be stressed here, though, that while this *shikaku seido* has been theoretically accepted and introduced in many companies, its realization in daily practice has turned out to be a tough venture. For example: managerial as well as common employees may be supposed to be regularly evaluated on their *potential* value for the company, on basis of which evaluation the *potential* level is to be determined (i.e. the kind of work and responsibility they *might* be entrusted with). In actual practice, this *potential-appraisal* often turns out to be quite a headache for most concerned, so that it becomes no more than a mere formality and its outcome questionable at best.[1]

More about personnel appraisals

Compared with his western counterpart the Japanese employee has a relatively vague definition of his duties and responsibility. 'The traditional assumption of an individual's role in an organization is that each must contribute his maximum to the organization's goal. No matter what his special abilities or particular assignment may be, he is expected to do his best in whatever position he happens to be at a given time. Stated another way, there is no impersonal, objective standard of performance. Instead, each individual's maximum capacity provides the standard against which he will be evaluated on the job.'[2]

Recently, management circles have attempted to define job requirements more clearly and in fact the *shikaku seido* opens up the possibility to proceed in that very direction. But in practice such developments have not been very successful so far. One of the problems seems to be the difficulty for most Japanese superiors to make an objective evaluation of the capacities (and potential) of their subordinates, while the Japanese tends to 'pay more attention to and find greater interest in personality than capability.'[3]

This latter view is substantiated by the data in the following example of appraisal practices in certain manufacturing firms (involving over 1000 regular employees). Generally speaking, the data (see table 6) seems to be quite in line with the usual practice in many Japanese companies, (viz, while attention is paid to work performance and capabilities, a great emphasis is put on the more subjective and personality-related factors.

Table 6

PERSONNEL APPRAISAL PRACTICES AT A MANUFACTURING COMPANY (1974)

	Work performance	Working attitude	General dedication	Shown ability	Personality	Potential (judged) ability
Promotion appraisal (1 per year)	XX	X	X	XX	XX	XX
Salary assessment (1 per year)	X	X	XX	XX	X	—
Bonus assessment (2 per year)	XX	XX	X	X	—	—
Self-appraisal and personal observation by superior (2 per year)	X	X	X	X	XX	XX

XX—great relevance   X—some relevance

Considered in more detail (see table 6), a superior involved in *promotion appraisals,* does not only look at the actual work performance, but also gives quite a lot of weight to demonstrated ability, personality, and potential ability. (The actual practice reveals that only a very few individuals move up the promotion ladder with extraordinarily high or low speed, while the great majority receives fairly automatic and yearly advancements, based on seniority and dedication', with little attention being paid to work performance).

In the case of appraisals relative to *salary assessment,* it is not so much work performance, but rather general dedication and proven ability that are said to play a major role in the decision. (The individual's basic pay is usually determined within the so-called *range-rate,* i.e. the permissible range of deviation from the standard wage increase curve. The basic wage is felt to represent the employee's personal prestige and standing within the company; the range rate is not wide and the actual amount of the basic wage of most employees in fact falls on the standard wage increase curve, while the majority of employees receive a 'special mention' with a remarkable regularity so that almost all keep about the same pace over the years. And yet, however small the differentials in levels of basic pay are, they often do provide clues as to the relative standing within the firm that may in the long run make a difference in treatment, e.g. the promotion to supervisory posts, re-employment after retirement, etc.). Then, there is the twice-a-year *bonus-assessment:* here the actual work performance may be given relatively more weight, be it that subjective and personality-related factors certainly are not overlooked, while, once more, in actual practice the distribution of bonus amounts usually turns out to be a largely automatic affair.

Finally, the *self-appraisal* and the *supervisor's personal observation,* focus on personality and potential ability. It is difficult to evaluate the exact nature of these appraisals as to their actual effect within the organization, except for the fact that again the work performance receives only scant attention. All in all, the data contained in Table 6 seem to support the above-quoted statement that the Japanese tend to 'pay more attention to and find greater interest in personality than capability', in spite of a score of official pronouncements to the contrary (like 'our remuneration system is based on work performance only', or 'seniority is on its way out in our company').

The same point is made by the following Ministry of Labour data. (In spite of apparent indications of belief in the 'work-centred' approach', it seems safe to keep interpreting this data as confirmation of the seniority-based system of promotion.) According to this survey [4] of almost 47,000 companies, the results of personnel evaluation were reported to be used for the following objectives. In over

38,000 firms, for the assessment of bonus amounts; in over 27,000 firms for the assessment of remuneration, excluding bonus; in over 23,000 firms, for promotion decisions; in over 20,000 firms, for suitable distribution of personnel, and in over 5,600 firms for training purposes.

Finally, it may be added here that most companies attach more importance to work performance in the case of blue-collar workers than in the case of white-collar workers where personality variables possess additional weight (see also sub Appendix 3).

Appraisals evaluated

In spite of the very widespread application of all kinds of appraisals, some experts hold that most personnel officials do not really know what to do with the results of employee evaluation in *actual practice*. For instance, according to Masahide Sekimoto 'In their merit rating forms they provide columns for evaluating capabilities or judging character, thus appearing to be up-to-date, but when they must actually evaluate an employee according to entries on his merit rating form and act on the resultant evaluation, they hesitate, wondering whether the merit rating system is truly useful in achieving stated aims. Indeed, I reviewed merit rating systems in some of Japan's largest companies and my observations supported my fears. Merit rating forms contained columns for evaluating capabilities and judging character, and entries were made periodically, but the resultant evaluations were either not utilized at all or utilized haphazardly ... I think my description probably applies to most merit rating systems used today in Japan.'[5]

Another expert highlighted the powerful informal organizational structure in Japanese firms as the main source of information about employees: within this context personnel officials would rather rely on the signals obtained via this network than through any kind of more 'objective' method for formulating promotion decisions about employees.

Similar remarks can be made about the application of more recent management techniques such as *management by objectives', 'self-appraising'* and so on. For example an Isetan Department Store brochure states that 'self-evaluation is taken into consideration at the term-end evaluation so that all employees may have a participation consciousness and the consent towards this evaluation system. The results of this self-evaluation will not be added to the evaluation marks, but will be taken into consideration at the time of evaluation by the superior ... It will be so arranged that when the desires of the employee and the necessity of the job fit together, personnel changes that can meet the desire of the employee can be achieved.'[6]

There are many doubts about the usefulnees of such techniques: where they have been introduced they have sometimes been received with enthusiasm, but more often they met with resistance, failure or indifference.

The role of the individual in the existing Japanese organization is different from the one in western organizations. As long as the old Japanese saying 'protruding nails will be hammered down' preserves its validity in Japanese society, it is likely that any management method which puts the individual at the centre of actual concern (i.e. independent from his group) will in the end have trouble showing the intended results.

Finally, it may be interesting to remark that a large majority of Japanese firms keep the rating results secret from the employees concerned. 'It may be even more astonishing to know that approximately half of all firms keep the results from supervisors. One wonders why they bother to conduct merit rating and, particularly, personality evaluations. In fact, keeping results secret is one cause for suspicion and distrust among employees toward merit rating.'[7]

Job evaluation and job classification

Time-study, job analysis and job evaluation and similar techniques are carried out relatively frequently in Japan, but still less than one might expect. For example, in a 1976 survey by the Labour Ministry less than 20 per cent of almost 7000 companies (including only about half of the very biggest firms) were reported to have completed some kind of job analysis on their premises.[8] Some firms report very elaborate job-evaluation programmes, elsewhere one is told of some relatively minor efforts in the same direction, or even that 'we just invented more modern-sounding labels for old practices' (in other words nothing much was done). Usually these job evaluation projects have been completely restricted to blue-collar levels, where the data obtained could influence part of the production employee's salary to some extent. Continuous technological change and increasing labour mobility have forced management to revise wage rates in a shift toward job-oriented systems and away from the traditional seniority-oriented system. These changes, however, do not mean a complete abolition of the traditional wage system: in most cases, the proportion of wages based on job evaluation accounts for only 20 or 30 per cent of the total wage income.[9]

In other words, in spite of serious efforts to create a more direct link between job classification and the categorization of personnel, the results have been quite limited so far and mainly restricted to blue-collar personnel.

Example of job classification: the case of Matsushita

Matsushita Electric Industrial Co. Ltd., is one of the companies to have introduced job evaluation at a relatively early date, as part of an effort to establish 'a new job-oriented compensation system'.[10] For manual workers, their jobs are classified on the basis of a point method. Evaluation factors are: knowledge (theoretical knowledge required for normal performance of the job), experience (length of experience based on theoretical knowledge), physical effort (arduousness of the work, tense posture and uniformity of movement), mental effort (over-attentiveness, monotony in combination with attentiveness and level and frequency of decision-making). The jobs to be performed in the category of 'manual work' are grouped into a number of *job groups* (eight line-worker-groups and two professional worker-groups). Weights, rating scales and points for specific job groups are determined according to the following schedule.

Table 7

EVALUATION FACTORS, RATING SCALES AND POINTS UTILIZED AS PART OF MATSUSHITA'S JOB-EVALUATION PROGRAMME: MANUAL WORKERS

Evaluation Factors	weight	Rating scales and points						
		1	2	3	4	5	6	7
Knowledge	15	15	45	75				
Experience	35	35	58	82	105	128	152	175
Physical effort	25	25	50	75	100	125		
Mental effort	25	25	50	75	100	125		

Source: Brochure: 'Personnel Management', Matsushita Electric Industrial Co. Ltd., 27.

Note: Specific definition and examples of jobs are given in each grade.

Per job group the successive maximum and minimum are determined for all jobs included. For example:

Table 8

MINIMUM AND MAXIMUM RATING POINTS PER JOB GROUP: MANUAL WORK (MATSUSHITA)

Job Group	Score Total minimum	maximum	Example of jobs
L1	—	171	Sweeping, simple packing
L2	172	213	Simple assembly work (soldering, etc)
L3	214	255	Complicated assembly work (inspector, etc)
L4	256	297	Chief of parts-assembly group; mass production on lathes
L5	298	339	Complicated adjustment of broadcasting studio equipment, semi-skilled miller
L6	340	381	Skilled miller, skilled lathe operator
L7	382	423	
L8	424		

Source: Brochure: Personnel Management, Matsushita Electric Industrial Co Ltd, 27.

About clerical and technical work, the Matsushita brochure is much shorter: 'Clerical and technical jobs are classified on the basis of grade descriptions. A whole job is compared by means of grade descriptions'. Supervisory work is dealt with very briefly: 'Supervisory jobs are classified on the basis of the title of administrative or supervisory positions'. About higher staff, i.e. section chiefs, department heads or higher, no further information is to be found in this brochure. Matsushita's job classification efforts seem to have been carried out most consistently at the blue-collar level.

The normal practice in most firms is to define very broad job categories, then to divide these into a number of job groups and in turn each job group into several grades, corresponding to subtle differences in wages and salaries. Yearly automatic promotions take place, which implies that an employee steps up one grade every year. Actual promotions are realized by 'jumping grades', which, however, also seems to be a regularly recurring experience for most employees (every few years; see also next chapter).

The least one can say about job classification is that it certainly has added a new dimension to Japanese personnel management (just like and in connection with systems of classification as the shikaku seido). Before its introduction only very broad categories had existed, largely undifferentiated, and employees were classified exclusively along educational and seniority lines for the performance of any duty which might show up in the work situation. Now more systematization has been introduced in company training schedules and the possibility has been created—even though not frequently used yet—to assign specific duties to particular people on the basis of more 'objective' factors.

Generally speaking young and rapidly expanding firms have been the most successful in adopting a 'work-centred approach of classification and remuneration' but it is said that the more traditional status classification almost invariably gets a foothold once the organization starts consolidating its position or has to slow down its tempo of expansion or gradually sees its labour force grow older.

Identity and change

Even though—in principle—recent developments open up the possibility of introducing more job-centred personnel policies in Japanese management, they are still largely based on traditional value judgments. Seniority, for example, seems to have preserved its essential validity. In the daily management practice there is no reason as yet to assume that American or other foreign management techniques are about to take over.

'Whereas in foreign companies it makes no difference who performs a job since he is paid at the same rate as anyone else who does the same job, in Japanese companies *who* performs a job is the determining factor in remuneration.'[11] Workers who perform virtually the same sort of work, are paid differently because such 'status' factors as previous school attainment, age and length of service all vary.

Of course, one may wonder whether it is at all necessary for the Japanese to completely revise their promotion policies and rigidly adopt western-style management practices. In spite of numerous far-reaching changes with a very direct impact on the lives of all Japanese, it is more than likely that Japan will preserve her essential identity and fare well by it. How this identity might manifest itself, is extremely hard to foresee; yet it is very unlikely that Japan would soon start to grow into a copy of any other industrialized nation, except for superficial appearances. 'In assuring that Japanese industry avails itself of the most efficient management, more and more emphasis is going to be placed on developing objective standards as to which foreign managerial attitudes are to be accepted and which refused; which traditional values retained and which discarded; and in the arena of evolving managerial techniques, which new developments should be applied.'[12]

Such development would be no more and no less than a repetition of what has happened a few times before in Japanese history: a careful evaluation of foreign practices and adoption of useful elements into the already existing pattern.

1.   See also my *Blue-collar workers in Japan and Holland: a comparative study* (Meppel-Holland, 1977), p. 173.

2.   Whitehill A. and Takezawa S. *The other worker—a comparative study of industrial relations in the United States and Japan* (Honolulu: East-West Center Press, 1968), p. 102.

3.   Chie Nakane. *Japanese society* (London: Weidenfeld and Nicolson, 1970), p. 123—The Ministry of Labour in *Yearbook of labour statistics, 1975*, p. 54, reports a 1976 study among 7000 private enterprises with at least 30 regular employees; 72.3% said 'to enforce a personnel review'. Out of these firms 79.1% reported to practice an evaluation of work ability; 77.8% of work attitudes and 68.7% of work performance. Even these (as such not interpretable) figures seem to indicate a preference for the 'personality' rather than 'performance' factor.

4.   *Yearbook of labour statistics, 1972* (Tokyo: Ministry of Labour, 1973), 56-7.

5.   Masahide Sekimoto. Japan's employee merit rating system in *Readings on managing employees* (Tokyo: Asian Productivity Organization, 1971), p. 3.

6.   *Outline of job-centred new pay system—for creating a new climate worthy to work* (Tokyo: Isetan Company Ltd. and Isetan Labour Union), 23, 27.

7.   Masahide Sekimoto, *Op. cit.,* 25-6.

8.   *Yearbook of labour statistics 1976* (Tokyo: Ministry of Labour, 1976), 54.

9.   Kazutoshi Koshiro, *Japan Labour Bull.,* April 1, 1972, p. 15. It should also be noted that the recession years 1974-76 revealed a tendency in the opposite direction: in 1976 older employees got relatively higher wage raises than their younger colleagues.

10.   The information concerned was obtained in printed form in 1972 and 1974 but the introduction of the 'job-oriented compensation system' was initiated well before those dates.

11.   Hirono R. In *The Japanese employee* Ballon R. ed. (Tokyo: Sophia University and Tuttle, 1969), 258-64.

12.   Noritake Kobayashi. Guide to a comparison of Japanese and American managerial effectiveness. In *Readings on managing employees* (Tokyo: Asian Productivity Organization, 1971), p. 31.

Reward   9

Regular monthly earnings

This chapter deals with direct remuneration in Japanese industry, i.e., with the cash rewards typical of wage and salary practices today; the next chapter will deal with what could roughly be termed compulsory and voluntary welfare benefits.

Official legislation states that wages are to be paid at least once a month and in cash. Bonuses and similar extra payments do not have to be paid every month. Most firms pay monthly salaries to all their regular employees. In many cases the so-called *nikkyu-gekkyu* system is applied, i.e. monthly payments for blue and white-collar employees equally (sometimes lower white-collar employees are classified as grey-collars together with most blue-collar workers).

The average monthly earnings of the Japanese employee can stand comparison with north-west European standards, an aim which was explicitly formulated in the early 1960s. Japan's per capita income is still relatively low, but it is improving rapidly though critics point towards the poor quality of life and the incredible environmental pollution as part of the heavy premium Japan had to pay for realizing this goal.

While the earnings of regular employees consist of a *basic salary*, along with a variety of cash allowances, non-cash provisions and some deferred payments (like the half-yearly bonus and the retirement allowance), one should be aware of the importance of the *basic salary* under conditions of lifetime employment security and seniority promotion. As a matter of fact, the basic salary is the direct expression of an employee's relative status within the company's hierarchy: it reflects his rank in the *shikaku* system of personnel classification.

In the context of this book it would take one too far to explore the composition of wages and salaries into great details. Appendix 3 provides an example of a salary composition which may be regarded as representative.

The system and composition of wages and salaries as such is rarely a matter for discussion between labour and management: negotiations deal mostly with amounts and percentages of increases within the existing structure and such increases are directly related to the financial situation and growth rate of the company within the total context of Japan's socio-economic evolution.

Every year management and company union negotiate a complete revision of the average amount to be paid for each job grade, thus creating a new structure of basic salaries. This complete upward revision is called the *'base-up'*: the basic salary goes up and with it most other cash payments. The *base-up* often consists of two elements: a percentage raise in basic salary and an absolute amount, a flat rate independent of age differences. Management tries to keep the percentage raise in basic salary as low as possible because this directly affects all future salary levels as well as bonuses and retirement allowances. If younger workers have a strong influence in the company union the absolute amount is likely to be higher: with fewer seniority years, their salary is low and they gain relatively more with a larger amount of cash than with a percentage increase, at least in the short term.

Labour-management negotiations deal mostly with average increases for specific subgroups within the basic salary structure, in addition to the cash amount which tends to be equal for all members of broader employee categories. The average basic salary thus frequently represents the earnings of the 'average employee', taking into consideration factors such as age and family responsibilities. The actual basic salary of an employee, therefore, falls somewhere within the *range rate,* an area of permissible deviation from the average basic salary (i.e. around the average of his own classification-group, usually ranging from 95 to 105 per cent). Negotiations often settle the leeway management is allowed in assigning raises to individual employees.

The base-up involves all job grades and does not reflect any real promotion; the same can be said about the seniority-based 'automatic promotion' (or *periodic increase)*: on the assumption that every year of service improves the experience and quality of an employee, a fairly automatic promotion is given to all personnel every year. This means that after all job grades have been revised in base-up negotiations everybody (in major firms at least) moves up one grade, merely because of seniority. [1]

After base-up and automatic promotion have taken place, an employee may be assigned to still a higher grade. Such *real promotion* is based upon superior performance, qualifications or personality or whatever factors management may consider to be relevant. As a rule most employees are promoted in this way every few years, the frequency of such raises being practically related to the level of school education completed before entering the company: the better the previous education, the more regularly such promotions do occur.

During the 1960s and early 1970s the starting salaries of school leavers have gone up considerably, mainly as a result of market mechanisms. Consequently a heavy strain has been put on the seniority-based remuneration structure which had traditionally been used. Table 9 shows how wage differentials have narrowed recently. From other sources one may also conclude that—in addition to seniority—the level of education also has lost part of its importance.[2]

Table 9

ABSOLUTE AND RELATIVE (STARTING SALARY OF HIGH SCHOOL GRADUATE=100)
BASIC SALARY DEVELOPMENTS IN 1961, 1970 AND 1975
MALE REGULAR EMPLOYEES ONLY,
IN COMPANIES WITH OVER 1000 vs 10-99 REGULAR EMPLOYEES
Absolute amounts × 1000 yen; relative in between brackets

| | Age | 1000 or more employees | | | 10-99 employees | | |
		1961	1970	1975	1961	1970	1975
Graduate of elementary or junior high school	-17	7.9 (100)	29.6 (100)	65.2 (100)	8.3 (100)	28.0 (100)	63.1 (100)
	18-19	13.2 (167)	41.8 (141)	87.8 (135)	13.2 (159)	39.4 (141)	80.5 (128)
	20-24	18.0 (228)	52.8 (178)	106.7 (164)	17.4 (210)	52.8 (189)	103.1 (163)
	25-29	25.7 (325)	69.3 (234)	132.0 (202)	21.9 (264)	66.3 (237)	127.5 (202)
	30-34	32.5 (411)	82.8 (280)	161.7 (248)	23.7 (286)	73.2 (261)	143.4 (227)
	35-39	40.7 (515)	90.3 (305)	178.6 (274)	27.7 (334)	72.8 (260)	149.8 (237)
	40-49	51.8 (656)	108.7 (367)	199.2 (306)	26.8 (323)	79.0 (282)	144.5 (229)
	50-59	50.4 (638)	108.4 (366)	199.4 (306)	24.9 (300)	71.4 (255)	141.5 (224)
Graduate of senior high school (old and new system)	18-19	11.6 (100)	37.2 (100)	77.0 (100)	10.1 (100)	34.7 (100)	75.5 (100)
	20-24	17.2 (148)	50.0 (134)	100.2 (130)	16.4 (162)	48.0 (138)	101.8 (135)
	25-29	24.0 (207)	65.8 (177)	127.4 (165)	23.8 (236)	64.6 (186)	130.7 (173)
	30-34	32.5 (280)	82.8 (223)	165.8 (215)	32.1 (318)	80.8 (233)	164.8 (218)
	35-39	43.3 (373)	97.9 (263)	190.8 (248)	37.2 (368)	88.2 (254)	180.3 (239)
	40-49	56.7 (489)	116.6 (313)	215.8 (280)	44.2 (438)	104.0 (300)	197.5 (262)
	50-59	67.2 (579)	144.5 (388)	276.7 (359)	42.6 (422)	108.3 (312)	207.3 (275)

Source: *Katsuyo Rodo Tokei, 1977 (Compendium of Labour Statistics 1977)* (Tokyo: 1977, Japan Productivity Center), p 52.

Note 1: absolute amount × 1000 yen.

Note 2: relative (in between brackets): starting salary high school graduate=100.

It may be interesting to note that in 1933 a senior high-school leaver received a starting salary which was 2.17 times higher than that of a junior-school leaver and a university graduate received about four times as much. Other data[2] show that compared with the starting salary of the junior high-school leaver, over the years the university graduate has lost relatively more and this trend of narrowing wage differences still continues. On the other hand—as shown in Table 10—the salary increase continues for the university graduate until he is about 55 while the progression tends to level off at about 45-50 for senior high-school leavers and even declines from about 45-50 for junior high-school leavers. This decline is most noticeable in smaller firms, less so in the big ones.

Table 10

EDUCATIONAL BACKGROUND, AGE AND AVERAGE MONTHLY EARNINGS: MALE REGULAR EMPLOYEES (OF 60,000 ESTABLISHMENTS SAMPLED): 1975.

(× 1000 yen)

Age	junior high school graduate		senior high school graduate		junior college graduate	university graduate
	production worker	salaried	production worker	salaried		
-17	65.9	64.2	—	—	—	—
18-19	81.2	81.0	89.4	82.5	—	—
20-24	101.4	103.5	105.7	101.6	103.7	105.8
25-29	123.5	129.1	127.5	129.4	130.1	133.4
30-34	142.7	156.7	151.7	161.3	167.0	172.7
35-39	150.0	171.1	162.1	180.8	190.7	212.1
40-44	152.9	178.9	163.1	196.0	207.3	242.2
45-49	154.1	189.3	163.2	206.2	256.9	278.8
50-54	152.2	193.2	164.1	217.2	277.7	301.2
55-59	130.3	166.0	136.1	185.5	223.1	254.5
60-	103.1	119.3	108.0	142.6	164.1	170.3

Source: *Yearbook of Labour Statistics, 1975* (Tokyo: Ministry of Labour, 1976), p 146-148.

I have pointed out earlier that company size is an important factor in personnel management patterns in Japan. As is seen from Table 11, employees in big firms not only receive higher wages but are rewarded more consistently along seniority lines as well. In small firms the seniority principle is abandoned from about the age of 40, while medium-size firms occupy some kind of intermediary position (with a peak in between age 40-44).

There are remarkable salary differences between various branches of industry, those with a high growth rate offering better financial conditions, particularly as far as starting salaries are concerned but the latter does not necessarily mean that then the whole salary structure of a certain industry is higher than average. For example, in 1971 the electrical machineries industry paid among the lowest starting salaries, but was among the companies paying relatively high salaries to their 55 year old employees.

Earnings also differ from one geographical area to another: the Osaka and Tokyo areas are known for their relatively high wages, while people in such far away districts as northern Honshu or Kyushu receive less for the same work.

Table 11

COMPANY SIZE AND AGE RELATED PROGRESSION IN AVERAGE MONTHLY
EARNINGS: 1975
(age group 20-24=100)

Age	1000 or more employees	100-999 employees	10-99 employees
-17	68	72	69
18-19	86	83	81
20-24	100	100	100
	(96.7)*	(90.9)*	(90.8)*
25-29	121	122	120
30-34	142	143	136
35-39	154	152	<u>139</u>
40-44	163	<u>154</u>	136
45-49	172	151	131
50-54	<u>180</u>	150	129
55-59	162	134	120
60-	103	109	105

* The average monthly earnings concerned, in absolute amounts (× 1000 Yen).

Source: *Katsuyo Rodo Tokei, 1977 (Compendium of Labour Statistics, 1977)* (Tokyo: Japan Productivity Center, 1977), p 51

Note: For size-related differences in absolute earnings: see tables 3 and 9.

Allowances (see also Appendix 3)

Except for the mostly quite substantial seasonal allowances (bonus), Japanese employees receive a broad range of other allowances, in addition to their basic salary. A number of these allowances are tax deductible, up to a clearly defined limit (e.g. the commuting allowance). A major distinction to be made is that between *duty allowances* (such as for supervisory work, for specific working conditions, shift and night duty allowance, etc) and *cost-of-living allowances* (such as the family allowance, housing allowance, commuting allowance, regional allowance).

In total, i.e. proportionate to the average monthly contractual earnings minus overtime, duty allowances accounted for 3.9 per cent and cost-of-living allowances for nearly 8 per cent of those monthly earnings in 1975.[3] Both percentages have shown a steady increase in recent years. Duty allowances are relatively more important in smaller firms; cost-of-living allowances clearly so in larger ones.

Without mentioning any further specifics, the following allowances were being paid in the indicated percentage of about 6000 firms (with 30 or more regular employees) in 1975.[3]

94

Duty allowances
supervisory post: in 80.4%
specific working conditions: in 16.1%
specific duty allowances: in 32.1%
skill allowance: in 38.8%

Cost-of-living allowances
family allowance: in 74.5%
regional allowance: in 17.1%
commuting allowance: in 86.7%
housing allowance: in 44.9%

Seasonal allowances or bonuses

In early years 'the semi-annual bonus, which was perhaps an adoption of foreign practice, was applicable only to company officers and managerial personnel. It seems that the practice then merged gradually with the traditional semi-annual gift presentation by the employer to workers. Around World War I production workers started collective bargaining on bonuses. Yet, until the end of World War II, bonus payment was generally viewed as a unilateral gift from the company.'[4] Thus in pre-war days the word 'bonus' was generally used to indicate a generous gift from management. Nowadays these extra half-yearly payments are considered to be part of the real wage, some unions even seem eager to replace the word bonus with the words 'seasonal allowances' to emphasize the change from a generous gift to a basic right. If not yet legally, practically speaking, the bonus is now regarded as an inherent part of an employees' salary.

Taira makes an interesting statement regarding bonus payments: 'In addition to the limitation of the "permanent" work force to a necessary minimum, the firm made its cost as flexible as was compatible with changes in the state of business. This was effected by the method of wage payments, which divided the total pay into two broad components, one of which was regularly paid and somewhat rigid, and the other was paid as a bonus or allowance adjustable to the state of business. Thus, contrary to an expected consequence of lifetime commitment—that labour is a fixed cost "not susceptible to adjustment as conditions require"—it seems that Japanese firms have on the whole maintained labour and wages as variable as conditions and economic calculus require. One would indeed suspect that by acceding to the unions' demand for job security, the employers might have obtained a greater degree of flexibility in production plans and work force management than possible otherwise.'[5]

Over the years the bonus payments have become a keystone for many Japanese households: it is usually spent on some durable consumer goods like a refrigerator, washing machine, a camera and so on. For employees of large firms the bonus varies between two to six months extra pay.

Negotiations about the amount of the bonus is one of the most important activities of the Japanese company-based union. On occasion unions have shown a delicate sensibility for financial problems of companies. After all who is to gain if too rigorous demands result in bankruptcy or at least in drastic cuts in future payment levels? The negotiations concentrate mainly on the total amount of bonus payments to be divided, on the average amount to be paid to certain groups of employees and maybe on some future guidelines for the distribution. Within these limits management determines the amounts to be paid to individual workers. One should keep in mind, though, that Japanese managers are hesitant to make too sharp distinctions among the people they have to work with and in practice bonus amounts tend to cluster nicely around the group's average amount.

Bonuses are paid half-yearly in June and December; summer bonuses tend to be lower than winter bonuses. At present, the average employee receives yearly three or four months' pay as bonus. The results of winter bonus negotiations often serve as an introduction to the coming 'spring wage offensive' in which labour and management confront each other all over Japan in efforts to determine working conditions and specially wages for the coming year.

Since bonuses largely depend upon basic salary and basic salary in turn is strongly related to company size, one should not be too surprised that big companies turn out to pay much higher bonuses to their personnel than small ones. But whatever the company's size, the bonus is a reflection of the company's performance in the immediate past.

Minimum wages at national level

Historically Japanese governments have been reluctant to intervene in labour market mechanisms by means of legally fixing a *minimum wage*. In April 1971 Japan ratified the Minimum Wages Conventions 26 and 131 but the minimum wage determination has been largely left to the employees' representatives and to employers. The government *is* represented in the so-called *minimum wage councils* in which the industrial partners discuss the level of minimum wages for specific industries, occupations and/or areas on an incidental basis. The acceptance of minimum wages may also be included in collective labour agreements. Japan does not operate a generally valid minimum wage level, but instead determines minimum wages for specific industries, occupations or regions (though in early 1975 the government promised to study the possibility of introducing a uniform, industry-wide minimum wage).

The traditional reluctance against government intervention in the determination of wages and salaries has extended into the present day. Japan does not have any clearly defined incomes policy, even though incidental price measures have been taken by the government. During the wage negotiations of spring 1975 the government urged employers not to grant any increases higher than 15 per cent; in 1976 this level was put at about 8 per cent, in 1977 even lower (be it very cautiously). The fact that the results of labour-management negotiations did in fact remain below this threshold (or just above it, as in 1977), was said to have greatly contributed to the government's success in the fight against inflation.

1. Even though 1976 reportedly showed an opposite picture, recent years have witnessed an inclination among managements to stop this seniority (or age) based periodic increase from about age 45 or 50. While this practice has become rather standard in smaller firms, recently also bigger companies are in the process of partially eliminating this automatic increase. See also chapter 4.

2. *Jokenbetsu Chingin Tokei, 1971* (Tokyo: Chamber of Commerce, 1971), p 35.

3. *Yearbook of labour statistics, 1975* (Tokyo: Ministry of Labour, 1976), 181-3. Excluded from these figures: attendance allowances, which were paid in almost 63 per cent of companies sampled, and amounted to one per cent of average monthly earnings (but up to 2 per cent in the smallest firms).

4. Whitehill A. and Takezawa S. *The other worker—a comparative study of industrial relations in the United States and Japan* (Honolulu: East West Centre Press, 1968), p 253.

5. Taira K. *Economic development and the labour market in Japan* (New York and London: University of Columbia Press, 1970), p. 187.

Welfare 10

Historically non-cash benefits have been an intrinsic part of per-sonnel administration under the system of lifetime employment security. Even before blue-collar workers were admitted to the status of regular employees they often received non-cash benefits like housing for single workers, working clothes, and one or two meals during working hours.

Early this century a great number of voluntary mutual aid associa-tions were established in many mines, factories and government offices, for the protection and welfare of the workers. Voluntary systems of retirement insurance appeared as well. Then, notably during the Taisho Era (1912-1926) a wave of paternalism brought about a considerable extension of employee welfare programmes, partly to secure a healthy work force and to prevent excessive turnover and partly as an expression of the then prevailing liberal mood among employers. Following the lead of industry the gov-ernment passed the Health Insurance Law in 1922 which still lies at the root of the present health insurance scheme. The Workmen's Accident Relief Law followed in 1931, the Unemployment Insurance Law in 1947, while the militarist regime promulgated the Welfare Pension Insurance Act in 1942.

Generally speaking, however, private industry had voluntarily established social insurance systems of its own well before the government followed suit. Partly as a consequence of these developments, the present social security schemes in Japan do not cover the whole population equally.

Health insurance

Health insurance is basically divided into two parts: *employee health insurance* for personnel of establishments where five or more people are employed and *national health insurance* which roughly covers all those who are not protected otherwise. The premium for employee health insurance (which is government-administered) accounts for 7.2 per cent of the declared earnings of the employee, in principle to be borne by employer and employee equally. Benefits include: medical care compensation, sickness or injury allowance, childbirth care and funeral expenses. Under certain conditions it is possible for larger firms to institute their own *health insurance society* with much better benefits than those provided by the government-administered system. While the premiums are the same as under the government scheme, on average, the ratio borne by labour and that by management is more favourable for the employees. There is a tendency for the employers' share to become bigger as the size of the organization becomes larger. In order to improve the health of employees (and in addition to what is legally mandatory), health insurance societies of big companies operate a great variety of such facilities as mountain lodges, seaside hotels, luxury health centres in hot-spring resorts, etc, where first-class service is provided to members and their dependents for really only a nominal charge. Especially the health facilities constitute a very important fringe benefit (compared to what is normally available), and are proudly announced in propaganda material for recruitment purposes. (In many cases, however, an employee loses his rights to any benefits when he retires from the company and does not get any refund of premiums paid.)

Most of the health-insurance societies in private industry are financially very sound—sometimes thanks to extra contributions from the company. The splendid resort facilities are but one proof of their strong position and from this point of view it is obvious that minor companies are at a big disadvantage.

In contrast, the government-administered employee health insurance scheme has been in the red for some years now, not unlike the health insurance plan for employees of small businesses (also government-administered).

Unemployment insurance and workmen's accident compensation insurance

Since 1972 these two forms of social insurance have been brought together under the Labour Insurance Law.

Virtually all enterprises compulsorily participate in the government-administered system of *unemployment insurance,* thus being obliged to protect their personnel against the hazards of involuntary unemployment. The premium consists of 13/1000 of the insured person's total monthly earnings to be borne equally by employer and employee. Like most social insurance premiums the employee's share is directly deducted from the monthly payments. Benefits may be received after premiums have been paid for at least six months before the day of separation.

The *workmen's accident compensation insurance* is a direct consequence of the Labour Standards Law of 1947 which holds the employer liable for employees' injuries or illnesses caused at the place of work. Hence, employers bear the full burden of premiums for this insurance.

Since 1972, coverage under workmen's accident compensation insurance is compulsory for all enterprises under the Labour Standards Law. The employer pays a premium based upon his payroll, the contributions amounting to at least 0.4 per cent of all earnings. The amount to be paid is determined by industry, depending on the frequency of accidents and on top of this the Labour Ministry which administers the scheme may fix a special premium for a company, taking into consideration its accident rate over the past three years. There are five kinds of benefits under this insurance scheme : medical care compensation, compensation for temporary disability, compensation for long-term disability, compensation for permanent disability and compensation for survivors plus funeral expenses benefits.

Major companies often complement the benefits under the workmen's accident compensation, be it to a less conspicuous extent than they do with medical-care facilities.

With the possible exception of the health insurance, Japan's system of social security has not as yet developed to any great extent. Thus being a regular employee of a large company not only provides the guarantee of lifetime employment, but also a wide range of social security provisions which extend into every major aspect of life. Whoever has not obtained the status of regular employee in a big firm, therefore, will have to face eventualities of life with much less security: the public system of social insurances still offers meagre prospects to those who have to rely on it exclusively, and those are many. (The national old age pension system was referred to in Chapter 4 ; see also Appendix 1.)

Voluntary fringe benefits : a broad variety

If we now consider *voluntary welfare provisions* (non-obligatory fringe benefits) the showing of major firms is certainly impressive whether compared with their international counterparts or with smaller enterprises in Japan. The word 'voluntary' must be properly understood : these provisions are not required by law but often they have been instituted at the unions' explicit requests. Originating in the special provisions for *shokuin* and the subsequent wave of paternalism in the early 1900s, and initially aimed at securing a steady and healthy work force, such provisions have come to be considered as a right, being part of the rewards for labour. It has been said that the present 'welfare-enterprise-ism' is not the same as the pre-war 'paternalistic familyism'[1] but the origin of present provisions undoubtedly lies in pre-war practices.

Recent reports suggest that younger employees are no longer interested in extra welfare provisions but prefer additional cash. In my view this is only partly true in that younger workers do not have to depend any more on their company for entertainment facilities as used to be the case ; rather the young generation favours a change

in the kind of welfare provisions they want, attaching more importance to housing provisions or loan facilities.[2]

Meanwhile 95 per cent of all companies explicitly help their personnel to participate in sports or other recreational activities, many
of them providing extensive sports facilities including gymnasiums,
playgrounds, table tennis halls and swimming pools. Sometimes
these facilities are open to the relatives of workers as well. By far the
majority of all non-school sports clubs are based in (mostly the
larger) companies, while public facilities also constitute only a
minute proportion of all gymnasiums or swimming pools in the
country.[3]

Many companies send employees to special courses to be trained
as recreational leaders, or even hire professional sports leaders. In
addition to the normal recruitment quota, some firms have a selection target of 'so many athletes' every year, regardless of other
qualities (though this seems largely done for PR reasons).

Lunchtime breaks are extensively used for a variety of sports or
similar activities: ping-pong, volleyball, baseball, Japanese chess
or *go*. Finally, once a year many firms organize athletic meetings
widely publicized in the house magazine.

Like at most universities, clubs of all kinds are proliferating
throughout Japan's industry, ranging from radio ham through
English conversation, zen meditation to flower arrangement. Musi-
cal bands of all sorts are to be found as are hobby clubs of every
variety. Some firms set up courses free of charge for employees.
Where the free Saturday has been introduced, employees may explicitly be urged to spend this day for self-development, with the firm
providing the facilities. Some companies also operate travel agencies for the service of their employees.

Finally, a highly typical service is the marriage arrangement. Many
a superior seems to feel a responsibility for the proper choice of a
marriage partner for his subordinates and tries to act accordingly.
The company president and the direct superior commonly play
important roles at a wedding ceremony, for which the company
provides some financial or other assistance. (It is not unusual to
hear a manager complain that much of his costly time is absorbed
by ceremonial duties of wedding parties of junior staff. Attending
wedding parties of children of business connections is another part
of the executive's duties.)[4]

Housing subsidies

In Japan's industrialized and urbanized areas the housing shortage
is unbelievable, even if one takes into consideration the traditionally
intensive use of floor space, through which the living room and
bedroom are the same room. The quality of many dwellings is of low
standards and would certainly provoke very strong protests if workers in Western countries had to live under similar conditions. About

2,700,000 flats of old wooden apartments were recently estimated to exist all over the country, 1,000,000 in Tokyo alone. In these flats two persons on average live on approximately 11 square metres. Conditions are worst in private rental housing where rents are very high as well. A great many Japanese families live in such privately rented houses. The rents in public housing units amount to about one-half of those for privately rented housing, but because of the ever-rising land prices, the rents are steadily going up.[5]

During the early 1970s while land and construction prices went up, simultaneously construction of public housing declined and people who wanted to move out of their substandard private accommodation into better public housing saw their hopes smashed.[6] Where the housing conditions apparently cause such tremendous troubles one might expect employees to rely upon their company for betterment of their situation. Indeed, most Japanese enterprises do provide some housing service for at least part of their personnel.

A quite recent survey by the Ministry of Labour showed almost 75 per cent of a large sample of companies provided some housing for employees, about half of them making houses available for families, and one-third also providing a house for single persons or operating dormitories or boarding houses. The typical room in a dormitory is not very large and is shared by two or three persons, but the rent is very low and often meals may be obtained at reduced prices. The rent paid by employees for company houses or flats is also very low and some firms may also pay part of the charges for water and electricity. An employee who moves along the promotion ladder may accordingly live in several houses in succession, each one fitted to the stages of his career: thus the kind of housing occupied is a sharp indicator of the in-company status of the family head, certainly in the managerial strata.

Employees who do not live in company housing often receive a housing allowance (see also Appendix 3).

Loans

Larger companies may grant loans to their employees, under specific conditions and for specific purposes. The most common loan is that for buying or building a house. For example, in 1974 a large manufacturing firm was reported to grant loans of between Yen 3,000,000 and 6,500,000 (depending on the location of the work) to employees at least 30 years old or of at least ten years of seniority; interest rates were very favourable and repayment had to be completed within 15 years.

Loans may also be granted for other purposes: for repairing the house, for university education of children, for marriage or for emergencies at home.

Many Japanese companies (again mostly the larger ones) encourage their employees to have deposit accounts with the company, often giving interest rates as high as twice those of ordinary banks. Of course, all such savings are voluntary but in practice it may happen that part of the bonuses is converted into savings accounts when cash is not readily available; this may only be done after negotiations with the company union.

Some companies provide their employees with some kind of private insurance system, in most cases group life insurance for which the employer pays the premiums. Again virtually all larger firms offer this kind of special benefit to their personnel, small firms much less so (partly because they cannot muster the minimum required number of participants).

Miscellaneous fringe benefits

A great number of payments in kind can be categorized as 'living assistance'. Virtually all major plants and most smaller ones offer some kind of eating facilities. Sometimes this is just a room where employees may eat their own food; about one third of companies operate dining halls where employees can buy cheap meals; some firms give their personnel a meal allowance.

Many firms provide their employees with proper work clothing, including shoes, helmet and gloves, and clean and repair these. In certain branches of industry the egalitarianism in clothing has gone so far that the way of dressing alone does not serve as a distinction between blue and white collars any more.

The inclusion of the following kinds of 'fringe benefits' in a category 'miscellaneous' does not imply that they are of minor importance, certainly not the health provisions and expense account.

Extra health provisions, in addition to those required by law, have been mentioned earlier. Their significance cannot lightly be overrated. Regular health checks for all personnel are the rule in many enterprises as well.

At least once a year some kind of social event will be sponsored by the management. In particular, the *bonenkai* or 'year-end forgetting party' (which literally is to forgive and forget the wrongdoing of the past year) is quite a common occurrence in Japan. On such occasions the men drink and boast a lot but many Japanese seem to stick to the adage that what has been said 'under alcohol' is to be forgotten later.

An old Japanese saying is 'he who is in good health and is always away from home makes a good husband'. In that sense a great many Japanese white collars make good husbands: it is estimated that the average white-collar employee spends over two evenings per week away from home on 'duty' for his company in a bar, restaurant or night club. For many *sararimen* the evenings on duty are said to be a welcome occasion to stay away from home: Japanese husbands are not much involved in the education of their children, most of them do not have much to say in home affairs, the average Japanese home is not very comfortable and many wives do not seem too eager to have the husband around too often. 'Japanese men enjoy informal talks with friends in bars or restaurants rather than at home . . . Thus a man spends not only the working hours but many evenings of relaxation in company with his colleagues; such close intimacy between working colleagues leads to the development of cliques and complicates the process of decision making.'[7] The younger men often join their boss or senior colleagues in social talks (frequently on company expense account), the older ones more often will accompany important guests, Japanese or foreign. A cautious estimate puts the number of hostesses in Japan at around 750,000, the majority working in bars or restaurants which almost exclusively depend on clientele from one or a few companies. 'Japan is a paradise of expense accounts. For one thing, the sky is the limit when it comes to entertaining a visiting VIP from abroad; his main concern, the contract he came to sign, seems forgotten in the whirl of social life. As for Japanese businessmen themselves, they regularly discuss and conclude important deals, and even less important ones, in the friendly atmosphere of restaurants and golf courses. The difference from the West is probably that expense accounts are not looked upon as a sales gimmick easily abused, but are an acknowledged means of maintaining in the business world and in society at large an expected standing that cannot be defrayed out of earnings.'[8]

In many enterprises senior officers and even lower ranking employees may spend more than their monthly salary for entertainment every month. The privilege to make use of an expense account, and to which extent, is a sharp parameter of an employee's company status and therefore also a determinant of his social standing outside the company. Apart from entertainment in bars and geisha houses, there is the habit of doing business at golf courses. Most managers are supposed to play golf regularly whether they like it or not and it is normal for the company to pay membership fees, which can be outrageously expensive.

Average monthly expenditures for welfare benefits

In 1975, the Ministry of Labour conducted a survey among about 6000 establishments, in order to determine the average monthly expenditures per regular employee for obligatory and non-obligatory welfare benefits, in various branches of Japanese industry. To cite a few of the findings [9]: in the mining industry, the average expenditure (per month) for obligatory welfare costs was 34.961 yen per company, as compared with 13.349 yen for non-obligatory costs. In the construction industry, the corresponding amounts were 19.836 and 4.608 yen; in manufacturing they were 18.112 and 6.320 yen; in finance and insurance 21.606 and 9.665 yen; and in transport and communication 18.627 and 4.997 yen respectively.

Following breakdown for the *manufacturing* industry may give some insight into the kind of expenditures involved.

Obligatory welfare costs (in yen)

health insurance contribution	4.743	workmen's accident compensation	1.197
welfare pension contribution	4.356	children's allowance contribution	138
employment insurance premium	1.313	others	38

Non-obligatory welfare costs

Company housing	2.823	extra accident compensation	104
medical and health services	543	solatium (congratulations,	
cultural, sports,		condolence)	188
recreation facilities	715	aid to home owners	262
canteens and other food services	919	private insurance plans	103
	(+287)*	others	438
cost of life protection	116		

(These amounts refer to the average amount, paid per month per regular employee in the manufacturing firms covered in this 1975 survey.)

*Extra payments for meals and meal tickets.

1. Whitehill A. and Takezawa S. *The other worker—a comparative study of industrial relations in the United States and Japan* (Honolulu: East-West Center Press, 1968), p 83.

2. My own study sheds some extra light on the attitude of younger workers re these extra provisions. See my *Blue-collar workers in Japan and Holland—a comparative study* (Meppel-Holland, 1977), p. 161.

3. The playgrounds and gymnasiums of public elementary schools are available for the general public on Sundays and public holidays, though not many people actually use these facilities.

4. Arai S. *An intersection of East and West* (Tokyo: Rikugei, 1971), p. 82.

5. See *Yearbook of labour statistics, 1975* (Tokyo: Ministry of Labour, 1976), 302-5.

6. Moreover, a number of newly developed sites were projected at highly inconvenient locations and turned out to lack a number of basic facilities. In April 1977 the Japan Housing Corporation disclosed some findings of its own: over 27,000 of its units remained unoccupied for a prolonged period of time, mainly because of such reasons as described here. All this in spite of the housing shortage.

7. Chie Nakane. *Japanese society* (London: Weidenfeld & Nicolson, 1970), p 126.

8. Ballon R. in *The Japanese employee* Ballon R. J. ed. (Tokyo: Sofia University and Tuttle, 1969), 130-1. The post-1973 recession has served to temper such spending bouts a little bit, with 'business lunches' gaining importance.

9. *Yearbook of labour statistics, 1975* (Tokyo: Ministry of Labour, 1976), 206-7.

Work 11

Employment rules and collective labour agreements

The Labour Standards Law puts an obligation on every employer of ten or more persons to submit to the Labour Standards Inspection Office a set of *employment rules.* The law also explicitly defines the main points which at least should be covered in those rules.

Collective labour agreements take priority over employment rules; thus the extent to which collective agreements and work rules overlap is an indication of labour's power in the company concerned.

The formulation of employment rules is a management prerogative but the Labour Standards Law stipulates that the employer shall consult the union or the persons representing a majority of his personnel while drafting or modifying them. When filing these rules or amendments with the Labour Standards Inspection Office, he also has to submit a written statement reflecting the opinion of the union or representatives of the majority of his staff.

Company regulations (employment rules) tend to be very detailed; they are commonly printed and invariably make up part of the instructions given to newcomers.

The collective agreement is usually less specific and less comprehensive than the employment rules. Except for general working conditions, other subjects which are included in a collective labour agreement pertain to collective bargaining, union prerogatives, labour-management consultation, remuneration, etc. The maximum duration of a collective agreement is three years but unless another term is explicitly mentioned either partner may notify the other one of termination of the agreement in a written document, at least 90 days in advance.

Many collective agreements are formulated in very general, abstract wordings often borrowed directly from related legislation and vague enough to guarantee ambiguous understanding. In contrast to western-European practice of concluding collective labour agreements on a national scale, Japanese collective labour agreements are concluded by labour and management at the level of the individual plant. Traditionally also, such agreements cover only few, if any, specific matters in details, but instead their conclu-

106

sion rather could be said to mean the official recognition of the enterprise union as representing the work force, or part of it, with the right to negotiate on behalf of its members and the explicit formulation of a willingness to maintain good relations between union and management. But lately more and more topics are being covered in collective bargaining sessions: labour is extending its area of influence in an effort to obtain a stronger grip upon the total work environment.

In the case of a merger, a new company succeeds the legal status of the old one including its employment relations (much will depend upon the willingness of the unions involved to co-operate with each other, as inter-union aversions can effectively make intended mergers impossible).

Working hours

The present Labour Standards Law of 1947 defines a normal working day as having a maximum of eight working hours and a normal work week a maximum of 48 working hours. However, the trend towards fewer working hours is evident (see Table 12).

Table 12

TOTAL NUMBER OF HOURS AND DAYS WORKED PER MONTH, PER REGULAR EMPLOYEE (IN COMPANIES WITH AT LEAST 30 REGULAR EMPLOYEES: EXCLUDING THE SERVICE INDUSTRY)

	days worked	total hours worked	normal hours	overtime
1965	23.6	192.9	176.4	16.5
1970	22.9	187.7	169.9	17.8
1972	22.8	184.7	169.3	15.4
1974	21.9	176.2	163.1	13.1
1975	21.6	172.4	161.5	10.9

Source: *Katsuyo Rodo Tokei, 1977* (Tokyo: Japan Productivity Centre, 1977), p 117.
Note: The recession years 1974-75 show a dramatic drop in overtime work.

Bigger enterprises have taken the lead in gradually reducing the working week. What is more, while regular employees in larger firms earn significantly more than their counterparts in smaller-scale undertakings, in fact they work fewer hours. For example, personnel in firms with at least 500 employees, in 1975 worked on average 20.9 days and 166.6 hours (in 1972: 22.3 and 180.3), as compared with 23.4 days and 182.7 hours (in 1972: 24.2 and 193.3) in companies with 5-29 employees.

The dual structure prevailing in Japan's economy apparently not only is reflected in the inferior earnings of personnel in small firms, but simultaneously in their substantially longer working hours.

The special protective legislation for women as laid down in the Labour Standards Law, limits hours of overtime work to a maximum of two hours a day, six hours a week or 150 hours a year. With the exception of some specific occupations (waitress, telephone operator), women also are prohibited from working on night duty between 10 pm and 5 am or on rest days. All these legal stipulations may be among the reasons why women employees on average work less hours than their male counterparts. The sex differentiation is particularly notable in larger firms, less so in small ones. The latter include many family-owned undertakings where the difference between the sexes seems less pronounced as far as the working environment is concerned.

There are substantial differences in the total number of hours worked monthly per industry. For instance, while in 1975 the total working hours per regular employee averaged 189.7 in construction (22.8 days), it was only 161.6 in chemical products (20.9 days) and 163.9 in finance and insurance (22.4 days).

A day's work normally begins at 7.30 or 8 am, office workers starting later, 8.30 or 9 am.[1] Late arrival often seems to be seen as something which in the mass-commuting society of urbanized Japan cannot always be avoided, but it is regarded proper for the employee concerned to try and make up for the time lost before returning home at the end of the day. In most companies employees are not allowed to turn up too early for work (e.g. more than 50 minutes before starting time), neither to leave too late without a specific order to do so (e.g. 50 minutes after the official end of the working day).

The Labour Standards Law does not oblige an employer to allow for rest pauses for a working day of less than six hours. For a working day of six to eight hours at least 45 minutes must be reserved for rest, and one hour if the day exceeds eight hours.

Overtime

All those who have not reached the level of section chief, normally are rewarded for overtime work, special allowances being given to employees not entitled to overtime pay.

The legal minimum for extra overtime allowance is 25 per cent which in 1975[2] was paid for normal overtime work in more than 90 per cent of companies surveyed by the Labour Ministry. Almost one third of companies with at least 1000 employees paid 25-35 per cent overtime. There is no legal obligation to pay additional overtime on national holidays but 83.9 per cent of companies under study paid 25 per cent extra in 1973, and almost 16 per cent of these firms paid more. Finally, up to 100 per cent extra allowance is paid for work during the New Year's recess when most companies in Japan close down for a few days.

If overtime is worked on night duty (between 10 pm and 5 am) employers are legally required to pay at least 50 per cent extra (25 per cent for overtime and 25 per cent for night duty). Minors under 18 are not allowed to perform overtime work or night duty, except for a few clearly defined occupations.

The amount of overtime worked in Japanese industry is high (see Table 12), even though the post-1973 recession resulted in a considerable drop in overtime work. Critics of Japanese management point out that the average worker is required to sacrifice an important part of his day during periods of economic expansion, while he is also the one to see his earnings dramatically reduced as a consequence of drastic cuts in overtime hours during recession periods.

Finally, in spite of undeniable changes, many white-collar employees still seem to hold the traditional attitude that it would be impolite to quit a day's work before one's superior decides to do so.

Shift work

In 1975, only 16.8 per cent out of almost 80,000 establishments surveyed [3] operated some kind of shift system. About 20 per cent of manufacturing companies did so, but here (like in other industries) company size made quite a difference: of establishments with over 1000 employees 73.1 per cent had some sort of shift system, 32.3 per cent of firms with 100-900 employees, and just 13 per cent of companies with 30-99 personnel. Within the total manufacturing branch of industry, the following displayed a high occurrence of shift work systems: petroleum and coal products (59.4%); textile mill products (52.1%); non-ferrous metals and products (46.6%); pulp, paper and paper-worked products (45.2%). In the mining industry, slightly over 27 per cent of companies sampled operated a shift system, as compared with 85.5 per cent in the electricity, gas, water and steam industry; on the other hand, in only 2 per cent of over 10,000 construction firms such a system was in practice.

Three shifts were operated in almost half of the largest manufacturing firms (mostly based on three or on four groups), while the three shifts–four groups system was practised in 45 per cent of companies in the 'electricity, gas, water and steam' branch of industry. Yet, with the further exception of 'pulp and paper products' , the two-shift system was a somewhat more usual practice in most companies (occasionally in combination with the three-shift system being operated within the same firm), more specifically the two-shifts–two groups system.

Finally a shift of 24 hours was practised in almost 3 per cent of the sampled companies (8.8 per cent of the largest ones); particularly in 'transport and communication' (16.4%).[4]

The five-day week

The introduction of the five-day week of 40 working hours (to catch up with Western Europe) is a topic of widespread debate in Japan. Since it became the fashion to talk about improvement of welfare levels of the working population it has become a target for union leaders, business managers and politicians alike. The system of two days rest is gaining momentum but is not widely practised yet. In September 1976, for instance, only 23.6% of regular employees in companies with 30 or more regular staff worked under a system of two days of rest every week, while 26.4% of them had only one day off per week (the remainder operating under different systems, such as twice a month two days off). Company size is an important variable: just one rest day per week was granted in 10.6%, 36.6% and 63.1% of companies with respectively more than 1000; from 100-999; and from 30-99 regular employees, while two rest-days every week were given in respectively 30.2%, 8.4% and 2.5% of the firms.[5]

In order to speed up the introduction of the five-day week in private industry, the government started an experiment of its own in October 1976: 30 per cent of the public employees are given a free Saturday once a month. The government is expected to expand the scale of this 'experiment' and also to allow banks to initiate a system of Saturdays off (still prohibited by law). It is expected that by 1980 the five-day week will be common practice in Japan. When this happens, Japanese employees would on average get 129 days off per year, including holidays.

One may have one's doubts about such predictions, but it is certainly a fact that compared to only just a few years ago, the commuters' flow in Tokyo on Saturdays has become less hectic. Moreover, young people show an unmistakable preference for jobs allowing two rest-days a week.

Holidays

Japanese law prescribes 12 national holidays, which are days off for public servants. Since these days are for national celebration, firms do not have to grant the same holidays to their personnel. Most large firms close down on those days, contrary to smaller ones and shops of which many do not interrupt business. In addition, quite a few enterprises are closed for the New Year season and on special company holidays, such as founder's day. Some companies give their employees special holidays during the summer when the climate can be very sultry and oppressive. One should keep in mind that the holidays mentioned here do not necessarily coincide with paid vacation days: this depends on the collective labour agreement or employment rules.

In the late 1960s the Tokyo Chamber of Commerce surveyed employers' daily living conditions and their holiday practices. It was found that in an overwhelming number of cases employers devoted all their time to their work, 23.5 per cent not taking even one single rest day during the year and the remainder taking only four to seven rest days. Thus disregarding the way these employers spend their working days, one must conclude that their days of rest appear to be far less numerous than those of their employees.

Restdays other than o-shogatsu and o-bon (New Year and All Souls) were unusual in old Japan. The Japanese have no tradition of a religious sabbath and no custom of summer holiday except for schools. Quite a few Japanese employees do not take up their total share of annual paid leave. While most of the young employees do take the leave they are entitled to, it is from the level of foremen or supervisors that holidays are not taken completely. Some white-collar employees even declare a paid leave when they are so unfortunate as to arrive late for work. Most employees of all levels like to keep some days of paid leave in reserve in order to safeguard 100 per cent payments in case of short sick leaves: under the normal conditions of health insurance the payments for non-occupational sick leave do not exceed 60 per cent of standard pay, and this only after the first four days of sickness.

Many employees, particularly white-collar, feel that their future chances in the company would be seriously damaged if they were to take even half of their rightful holidays. In spite of frequent statements to the contrary, enjoying a large or even full share of annual holiday is considered to be something un-Japanese and a manifestation of egocentrism.

Not surprisingly, then, at the 54th International Labour Conference in 1970 the Japanese government voted against the adoption of a convention that three full working weeks should be granted as annual paid leave.

Several studies reveal the rather limited ability of married male Japanese employees to privately make use of their free time. Most leisure time is spent rather passively doing nothing, hanging around, watching television and this is explained by lack of money and the need to relax after today's work to be fit for tomorrow's! At the same time they display an outspoken tendency to spend their leisure time with colleagues. Many companies provide a variety of recreation facilities for them and their relatives. Consequently, much of the leisure time which an employee may afford will be spent under the company's umbrella with the very same people he works with and leisure tends to become a direct extension of company life.

The Labour Standards Law stipulates that the employer shall grant a number of paid vacation days to his employees, adding that these days may be given separately or at once. At least six days are to be given to employees who have worked for one year continuously with an at least 80 per cent attendance record. Then for all those who without interruption have worked for two years or more, for each consecutive year of employment one day of paid vacation is to be added, till a maximum of 20 annual paid vacation days.

While the typical practice traditionally has been and still largely is to take up a few vacation days at a time, in recent years it has become the custom to close down the plant to give all employees a holiday at the same time. Where this is not the case, employees tend to take more days off at a time than they used to, particularly the younger ones.

Personnel adjustment tools

Under conditions of lifetime employment Japanese management cannot easily discharge personnel when the economic situation seems to call for such an action. Of course those who work without the status of regular employee constitute the first bumper against economic fluctuations. In addition management can use a few tools of personnel adjustment which preserve the basis of lifetime employment but at the same time provide for the possibility to react flexibly when needed. Besides reduction in the numbers of new recruits the most notable adjustment tool is to be found in the widespread *intra-company mobility* by means of which part of the existing work force may be relatively easily transferred to those points in the organization where manpower can be better utilized.

Matters relating to personnel transfers (including appeal procedures available to employees) are stipulated in the collective labour agreement, occasionally in the company rules or in special labour agreements. Usually some reference is made to advance notification and to the way the union is to be involved in the decision-making procedures. In practice unions rarely object to transfers in the case of internal transfers within the same plant while transfers to different plants within or without the original concern could cause more trouble. Employees expect to be rotated and reassigned according to the requirements of production and management. A Japanese manager once told me that 'job demarcation here is very vague, so an employee has to accept a transfer, even if it makes his skill obsolete or useless ... the Japanese pattern of transfers is functional to a man's job and position, even though his present skill may become useless'.

Some firms carry out regular personnel transfers on a large scale.[6] This so-called *teiki-ido* is conducted every one or two years in order to shake up the whole structure, serve training purposes, refresh work patterns, correct weak points in human relations, respond to individual desires, etc. Frequent transfers guarantee a broad experience and usually mean rapid promotion of key employees.

In time of recession it is not uncommon for large companies to unload part of their personnel by means of transfers to a 'related company' which may be a subsidiary of the original concern or have some other important business relation with it. Neither the receiving firm nor the employee to be transferred has much chance to refuse co-operation, the former because of far-reaching business considerations, the latter because refusal would mean the end of his career.

Another tool of personnel adjustment is *voluntary retirement;* it is usually rewarded with an extra severance allowance. In the case of older employees (who may be requested more or less in person to resign voluntarily) this may mean that they receive about the same retirement lump sum that they would have obtained on reaching the fixed age limit. By encouraging voluntary retirement Japanese management wants both to reduce its manpower force and to uphold its commitment to lifetime employment.

In recent years more and more firms have (reluctantly) taken to some kind of lay off procedure: this includes the guarantee of a certain percentage of the employee's normal earnings and the promise to reinstate all the people concerned in their original jobs after a fixed period.

When for the sake of rationalization or some other reason a *merger* is deemed necessary, important personnel adjustment will be inevitable. In such a case, some firms require employees to resign voluntarily while in a small minority of cases superfluous workers are discharged. If workers are dismissed in larger enterprises they are more likely to be offered company-arranged new jobs than in smaller firms. Usually the company union will be co-operative, either to prevent even worse consequences or to gain a more powerful position through hoped-for increase of membership.

On the part of employees also there is a possibility to break with lifetime employment commitment: external mobility and absenteeism are not unfamiliar phenomena in Japan. *Labour turnover* is higher among younger employees than among older ones particularly in the smallest companies. The young Japanese is allowed to search around till he is about 25 after which he is supposed to have found the company where he will stay until retirement. Usually the employees have to notify management at least two weeks before they intend to leave.

Absenteeism, though on the increase, is still rather unusual in Japan, partly because of pressure within the group which would have to bear the consequences if somebody stayed away without previous notice. The most common means to combat absenteeism are a special allowance to encourage perfect attendance or some kind of financial penalty for absences.

Safety precautions

The casual visitor to any Japanese company must have noted the numerous *anzen dai-ichi* (safety first) signs and cannot evade the impression that safety and prevention of industrial accidents are in the focus of managerial attention. The frequency and severity of accidents is higher in smaller firms, bigger firms being very much concerned about their safety reputation and financially able to do more about it. Statistical data show that subcontracted and temporary workers are more likely to be involved in a serious accident than regular workers.

At plant level the execution of safety programmes is considered to be the duty of lower management in spite of the fact that the new Industrial Safety and Health Law puts the ultimate responsibility with the highest hierarchical levels. No clear-cut distinction is usually made between safety, health and hygiene. In large firms the medical department may be in charge of enforcing safety regulations, a medical doctor being frequently the head of such a department.

Critics of Japanese management often imply that it is inclined to blame the individual employee for accidents rather than the work environment, and that too much priority is given to fostering safety consciousness, instead of improving safety devices. It is felt by many people that the principle of 'production first' largely overshadows the one of 'safety first' in spite of all outward appearances.

Discipline

In comparison with their western counterparts, Japanese managers seem to be reluctant to formally discipline employees. Formal disciplinary regulations vary from one firm to another but usually five levels of punishment are identified: admonition or warning, restriction of holidays, reduction of salary, suspension from employment for a specified time with loss of salary, and finally discharge. In practice, punitive measures are rarely undertaken:[7] the rules are mainly applied against those employees whom management wants to get rid of. If someone, after the initial screening procedures still does not conform sufficiently, the lifetime employment system may become the ultimate reason why—in the management's view—he has to be weeded out.

While Appendix 4 provides a good example of disciplinary regulations (for blue-collar workers) in a major shipbuilding firm, a short note should be added about the processes of appeal. An employee has the right to appeal against any disciplinary action he is subjected to. Most companies have special appeal committees, composed of representatives of labour and management. When labour relations are strained, management may well be inclined to take disciplinary decisions without much reference to the union side, or perhaps seek the co-operation of the (presumably better disposed) second union (see at the end of next chapter).

Occasionally the injured party may go to court for a final appeal. It would be very exceptional for an individual employee to take such a step, but individual cases may be utilized for ulterior purposes, e.g., in order to expose certain practices to the public or to test specific legal points.

Even though on the increase in recent years, severe disciplinary measures taken by management in the private sector are very rare (although the public sector has displayed a more aggressive stance over the years: see the last chapter of this book). Generally speaking, Japan's industrial society prefers to resolve its problems informally, avoiding conflict whenever possible.

1. Systems of 'flex-time' are spreading gradually, in which employees can determine their own time of starting and ending work (everyone being present during specific hours, though).

2. *Yearbook of labour statistics, 1975* (Tokyo: Ministry of Labour, 1976), 254-5.

3. *Yearbook of labour statistics, 1975* (Tokyo: Ministry of Labour, 1976), 248-9. The survey covered only companies with at least 30 employees.

4. The 24-hour shift is a somewhat frightening practice that serves as a handy conversation piece with many a Tokyo taxi driver who works under such a system.

5. *Yearbook of labour statistics, 1976* (Tokyo: Ministry of Labour, 1977), 271-2.

6. Some companies, notably so in the travel industry, are almost notorious for the tempo and thoroughness of their personnel shake-ups, every six months or so. Thus, for an interested outsider, it counts as a particular challenge to try and predict 'who will be who', especially since personal acquaintance is so important in Japanese business dealings.

7 Except in the public sector, where in recent years thousands of employees have ignored the legal prohibition for them to strike. Subsequent disciplinary actions invariably resulted in renewed offences, etc. The Japanese National Railways seem to have presented the most-widely publicized case.

Relationships 12

Sempai-kohai

Highly personal, informal relations are a dominant feature in Japan, and not the least so in her major industrial organizations: in fact, informal connections have taken on such strongly emotional, but also functional connotations that they must be seen as an irreplaceable pillar of Japanese personnel management.

Informal groups, such as school cliques (graduates from the same university) or regional cliques have been mentioned before. Another powerful informal system is directly linked to the principle of seniority: the *sempai-kohai* relation. Japanese tend to be highly sensitive to differences in seniority which grant some implicit priority rights to the one with the higher seniority ranking (the *sempai*) over one with a lower ranking (the *kohai*). Even though this *sempai-kohai* relationship naturally applies to all regular employees in an organization, it is quite usual for a junior employee to build up strong personal ties with one specific *sempai* who, on average, is about 10 years older than him. These close mutual bonds are preserved over the years in spite of frequent transfers or any other changes and it occurs in all layers of the Japanese organization, but most particularly in white-collar and managerial ranks.

Why or how such a bond comes into existence depends upon several factors. Experiences at the start of his employment may make the young employee attach himself to anyone who can provide some guidance. The relative standing of the prospective *sempai* in the company, his influence, may be another factor, or a common university background, or connections between the two men's families. Even though a Japanese employee may affectionately refer to a number of seniors as his *sempai,* usually he will feel a highly exclusive attachment to just one particular senior.

The *sempai* relationship is based upon a deep sense of mutual obligations. The *sempai* will try to introduce his *kohai* into the 'company way' while providing him with protection, securing favourable assignments, advising him on the solution of problems, etc. It is no undue exaggeration to say that the *sempai* fulfils a father role, not unlike many professors (*sensei*) do for their students. The junior, on his part, will show his sincerity, support and defend his senior if needed and enhance his *sempai*'s status by all means available.

A *sempai* may have several junior employees who share such a deep personal relationship with him. The more influential a senior is, the larger the number of his juniors. Conversely, the more juniors attach themselves to a man, the greater his personal status within the total organization. Personnel transfers not infrequently are used to let informal *sempai* groups coincide with functional units of the formal organization. Where the leader's effectiveness depends largely upon the willingness of his subordinates to work hard for him, the ideal group in Japanese eyes may be the group where the leader is also the special *sempai* of his subordinates. On the other hand, in case of death of the leader or in case of his long absence, the *sempai* group may easily dissolve into rival factions; it is primarily the personal ties between juniors and seniors which hold such a group together.

In political life similar cliques are a well-known phenomenon, having an indelible impact upon Japan's political life; here the age difference seems to be less important than plain political influence, while changing loyalty is more common in politics than in industry. In both settings, rivalry between factions can be witnessed regularly.

Sempai groups may coincide with units of the formal organization, but frequently they will not and their influence may extend into every corner of the enterprise. The formal organization, therefore, is covered with a barely visible web of personal inter-relationships, which has a direct impact on the workings of the whole structure. Japanese refer to this widespread informal structure with the concept of *nemawashi,* an intricate root system with a myriad of almost invisible inter-connections all contributing to the functioning of the whole enterprise.

Leadership

Irrespective of whether or not a functional unit coincides with a sempai group, the Japanese leader is expected to care for the 'whole employee'. 'The Japanese are concerned with the employee and the product. Americans just care about the product. The Japanese appear very much to want the employee to be comfortable. I never get the impression that the higher-up Japanese managers don't have time to talk. They usually seem concerned, whereas American bosses convey a "you have to work, that's all there is to it" attitude.'[1]

Often Japanese refer to their own style of leadership as *wet leadership,* a style in which social skills are of major importance, along with personal attention for the employee as an individual with his own happiness and worries. Western *dry leadership,* on the other hand, is felt by many to be impersonal, too businesslike, coldly pursuing material profits. This does not necessarily imply that a Japanese manager would never be authoritarian or quite demanding as far as his subordinates' work is concerned: much can be tolerated of a leader if only he shows 'sincerity', a 'warm-hearted interest' for the personal affairs of his people. A warm style of leadership seems to prevail in the lower ranks of the hierarchy, while more authoritarian patterns may become more common higher up.[2]

The modern Japanese organization, largely founded upon the lifetime employment system as it still is, offers abundant explanation possibilities why 'wet' leadership is strongly preferred. Without the ready possibility of eliminating less favourable elements through dismissal, the company tries its best to select only desirable personnel, but once selection has taken place, it will try to reshuffle employees frequently in such a way that pleasant inter-personal relations are more likely to exist. The employee on his part, realizing that he is supposed to stay with the company for the rest of his life, will try to create a pleasant atmosphere, or at least, to prevent an overt clash with anyone. Thus, good relations and sociability become vital requirements if one wants to survive reasonably.

A very outstanding level of performance may even negatively influence a man's career. 'Any returns from the individual's contribution are enjoyed by the group as a whole, with the resultant prestige attributed to the leader; meanwhile the capable man who has made a significant contribution remains one of the junior members. His boss and his colleagues may well be aware of his distinguished contribution, but they take it for granted that it should be a matter of profit to them to have such an able member in their group.'[3]

The able subordinate, therefore, had better not claim too much praise for his merit, but instead show devotion to his boss in diverting the prestige to him; a good relation with the leader as the exponent of the group is mandatory. The Japanese group is not primarily based upon specialization and operates under conditions of collective responsibility rather than individual task descriptions. Performance, then, will largely depend upon willingness among the group members to co-operate and divide the work load in an acceptable way.

Under the still prevailing system of promotion, many superiors have not primarily climbed the ranks on the basis of demonstrated ability, but rather because of the way they can get along with people, in addition to their level of seniority.

On the other hand, many Japanese leaders in business and industry undoubtedly possess great personal managerial ability: they are the ones who act in a more authoritarian way and lay down the grand design within which the total organization is to function. However, among top managers today there are more than a few who spend most of their time waiting to approve proposals originated by middle management or acting as the firm's representative at numerous social occasions.

(Ringi) decision making

Clear-cut individual duties being mostly absent, decisions are taken in a continuously revolving process of deliberations, to be followed by formal consent or approval of all concerned : this is called the *ringi decision-making* procedure. As regards the work environment, most companies are characterized by huge open offices where middle managers work among their subordinates. Such a setting where many work groups operate serves to facilitate communication. The sense of collective responsibility and the close proximity of individuals within the group enables everyone to participate in most target objectives and general planning formulated by top management ; it also provides an incentive for everyone to be on the look-out for the best means to achieve them.

If a problem has been recognized somewhere in the middle-management layers, extensive energy is concentrated in gathering data concerning the problem area. The informal communication network will serve to facilitate contacts with people in other departments, across functional boundaries. Gradually, through much study and numerous talks with everybody who might conceivably have something to do with the problem, a proposal takes shape. It is then formulated in a document (*ringisho)* spelling out the problem and its possible solution. This document is then circulated at the same level in the hierarchy (horizontally) over several sections and even departments, after which it is submitted to consideration upward in the hierarchy (vertically), again over a number of sections and departments. Everyone who receives this document is supposed to study its contents carefully and to affix his seal to the document giving his formal consent. Disagreement can be expressed by sending the proposal back to the originator, stamping one's seal upside down, or comparable methods. When a proposal has formally passed through all appropriate hierarchical levels of the relevant departments, a top manager, often the president himself, will affix his seal : the proposal then becomes a decision and execution can start. Even though it is clear where the proposal has originated, throughout the whole *ringi* procedure there seems to be an almost deliberate effort to maintain vagueness as far as responsibility and authority are concerned.

The advantage of this system is that it gives junior staff the chance to influence management decisions and at the same time to share responsibility with a great number of seniors ; since so many people are involved the risk of blundering is reduced to a minimum ; the process of consensus building is likely to create a strong sense of identification with the proposal-turned-decision and the execution will take place at great speed.[4] One of the clear drawbacks of the system is that it is very time-consuming; high up in the hierarchy the many *ringi* documents offered for consideration tend to pile up and in addition the vagueness about responsibility and authority, inherent to the *ringi* procedure, contributes greatly to the rather frequent phenomenon of inefficient superiors occupying a place in the hierarchy while relying solely upon the efforts of their middle-management subordinates.

National consensus: the quality control movement

One example of Japanese decision making on a national scale was the *quality control movement* which started in the 1950s. Partially at the instigation of some American experts a conviction took shape among the leading industrialists and government bureaucrats that improvement of the quality of industrial products would enable Japan to gain a better foothold in the international market. Knowledge and expertise concerning quality control were introduced from abroad on a large scale and at high speed. With the arrival of the 1960s 'quality control' had become an indispensable notion in Japan's industrial society. The radio and television industry were extensively involved in imbibing the necessary knowledge. *Quality-control circles (QC circles)* came into being, their number expanding tremendously in firms all over Japan. By opening up the possibility of participation in QC circles to rank-and-file workers, management enabled them to formally engage in work which so far had been the exclusive and coveted domain of the 'higher ups'.

Nowadays, mostly employees at the lowest end of the hierarchy (foremen and lower) take part in QC circles or in comparable group activities; membership is voluntary, meetings do not take place during working hours and usually no direct financial reward is given for participation.

The growth in participation rates in QC circles and similar activities has been tremendous. The remaining non-participating minority has come to be frowned upon as lacking proper dedication, a direct threat to the original spontaneity of these movements. Recent developments indicate that participation on the work floor may increasingly be realized through regular sessions organized for and attended by all members of the work group, during normal working hours. One example is the 50-minute Friday meeting at Mitsubishi Koyagi Shipyard in Nagasaki:[5] rank-and-file members discuss how to attain certain targets, mostly given by management through the foreman or sometimes set by the group members themselves. How far such more formalized group meetings would come to replace the more spontaneous participatory actions (as QC circles), remains to be seen. But no doubt, participation at grass roots level (on the work floor) in Japanese industry has developed to such an extent that it deserves wide attention.

Suggestion systems and company journals

Almost all major firms operate some kind of suggestion system for their personnel; this practice is also quite popular in the smaller companies. Ideas may be submitted by individual employees and by groups. The suggestion system is used intensively (much more than in the USA or in Europe and with better results), and the procedure of evaluating and rewarding the suggestions includes one or several committees consisting of management and employees' (usually union) representatives. Some firms hold regular exhibitions of suggestions that were selected and implemented.

Outstanding suggestions are also reported in such communication media as company papers or house journals which have attained widespread use in Japan. Another means of information channelling is the information board which can be found in almost every corner of a Japanese plant, providing data on safety records, comparative performances data, vacancies, special holidays and overtime regulations, policy decisions, etc.

Grievances, committees and joint consultation

Throughout the domain of communication and participation in Japanese industry, there is a clear, obvious preference for *informal* procedures.

This holds true for the way *grievances, complaints and conflicts* are usually dealt with. Formal complaint procedures are rarely followed; most grievances are resolved within the work group, informally. The same can be said of vertical relations with higher supervisory and managerial levels: the mighty informal strength of the organization will be used as far as possible, to mend breaches of mutual trust. And if committees are established to study a particular problem, its workings will tend to be heavily dependent on informal mechanisms, as well.

Actually, the inclination of the Japanese to work in groups without clear-cut responsibility patterns may provide one explanation for the proliferation of *committees* in Japanese companies. It is very difficult to describe the actual practice of such committees, because of the huge variety of their composition, working procedures, stated purposes, etc. There are committees established to deal with specific technical problems, a new technology, relations with a certain (foreign) customer, analysis of statistical data, and so on. In committees like these, the basis is laid for the amazing thoroughness and preparedness with which Japanese usually enter negotiations.[6] In spite of their ubiquitous presence, most of these committees are not based on legislation, or other specific formal regulations.

One salient example is the *'joint consultation'* process: even though Japanese law only guarantees labour's right to bargain collectively and nothing more, one of the more important activities of enterprise unions is the participation in joint consultation with management in some sort of institutionalized meeting named 'management conference' or 'joint consultation council' or something of the sort.

After the Pacific War, many enterprise unions had obtained considerable power to decide on matters relating to planning, production, etc. As management gradually strengthened its grip again, the practice of joint consultation came to be institutionalized as a way of keeping the official employee representation interested in the company process and of securing their co-operation in carrying out unpopular measures.

In this way the joint consultation practice spread all over (major) Japanese industry, in spite of the absence of any legislation concerning a 'works council' as is found in some West European countries. At present, the 'management conference' (or whatever its name) exerts many of the powers that by law have been given to its West European counterparts. One important difference remains: the absence of a legal foundation for joint consultation makes the possibility of undue management influence greater than elsewhere.

Most unions in Japan are company unions, they are highly autonomous units whose membership consists entirely of regular employees of the company concerned (below the level of section chief, see next chapter). In the joint consultation process, employees usually are represented by officers of the enterprise union (who themselves are employees). They may receive some confidential material that is not normally accessible to the rank and file.

In the consultative meetings, a whole variety of topics may be discussed, mostly matters regarding working conditions and managerial or production issues. During some sessions, management just explains future plans, on other occasions advice may be asked on specific issues, while still other meetings take the form of informal get-togethers for exchanging views and information. (A high-ranking manager once told me he spent more than half of his evenings with informal outings or meetings with union officials, considering these contacts as essential for the good of the company.) Actually, one ought to consider the joint consultation practices as a year-long preliminary to official union-management negotiations:[7] at the consultative level no formal collective bargaining takes place yet, and no right to strike exists. If no definite consensus can be reached during these consultation sessions, then only may one formally resort to collective bargaining and threaten to strike, or an arbitration procedure may be started. At any rate, both management and many unions in private industry prefer harmonious labour-management relations to confrontation.

The second union phenomenon

Joint consultation procedures may work excellently under conditions of fundamental harmony between labour and management but they tend to run awry where adverse conditions prevail. At times in the public sector and occasionally in the private sector labour-management relations can and do turn sour. Under such conditions, the well-tried mechanism of joint consultation is likely to falter or break down, complaints about unfair labour practices become more common and courts may be requested to decide on legal issues. Management confronted with strained labour relations will try every means to bring relief in such an adverse situation. One solution may be found in the so-called *second union.* If management has reason to believe that the union's leadership rather than its members are unwilling to co-operate, efforts may be initiated to find reliable employees to start a union of their own. Once the first formal steps have been taken by these reliable employees management may feel free to express its preference for the new union and extend all kinds of favours to its leadership and members in contrast with the original union. In practice it has been found that most second unions succeed in attracting the majority of eligible regular employees as members within a few years.

1. Johnson R. T. and Ouchi W. G. Made in America (under Japanese management). *Harvard Bus. Rev.,* Sept-Oct 1974, p 67.

2. Whitehill A. and Takezawa S. *The other worker—a comparative study of industrial relations in the United States and Japan* (Honolulu : East West Center Press, 1968), p. 169.

3. Chie Nakane *Japanese society* (London : Weidenfeld and Nicolson, 1970), p. 49.

4. Compare my own findings in my *'Blue-collar workers in Japan and Holland—a comparative study* (Meppel-Holland, 1977), 126-7 ; 224. In western countries where much less participation is observed in the process of decision making, it seems that identification with the decision is bound to be lower and therefore its realization slower, though the decision itself is taken much more quickly.

5. As we found being practised during a study tour in 1974. See our: *Werken in Japan* (Assen-Holland, 1975), 16-22 ; and also: Japan : maatschappij en medezeggenschap in het bedrijf. *Intermediair,* vol. 10, no. 30, 26 July 1974.

6. At least if developments are predictable, as is often the case in negotiations with prospective trade or industrial partners (note that expatriate offices of major import-export firms, as well as JETRO, tend to serve as significant 'data banks' concerning such potential partners. In international politics, it seems, the Japanese often come out rather unprepared, or awkward. A notorious example was the 1977 fisheries negotiations with the U.S.S.R.

7.   The joint consultation process may be formally concluded with a few bargaining sessions, of which the outcome may be pretty well known to the representatives, before such meetings have even begun. An excellent example is to be found in the pay increase offers made by managements in the steel sector in April 1977; newspapers reported off-handedly that they had been agreed upon, long before the official bargaining started.

Organized labour 13

Historical background

In spite of efforts on the part of labour leaders the power of labour unionism was never very impressive before the Second World War. Even the more moderate unions advocating a policy of collaboration with management in order to gain some improvement in working conditions, met with strong opposition

Where radical political ideologies gained the upper hand, outright harassment and police brutality made the struggle even more difficult, with a concomitant estrangement from the working masses.

At its peak, the rate of labour organization in prewar Japan reached eight per cent of the total labour force. From the late 1930s onward the increasingly hostile government policy made the labour movement virtually disappear, to be replaced finally by the *Sanpo* (Association for Service to the State through Industry). This government-controlled organization came to include all employees within most companies, from top management down to the lowest blue-collar worker, and was based upon units coinciding with separate factories (the immediate predecessor and model of postwar Japanese company unionism). The ultimate purpose of this militarist body was, of course, total involvement of each and everyone in an all-out effort to increase productivity for the sake of national goals.

After the war for the first time in its history, Japanese labour was given unequivocal protection, at least initially, by legislation guaranteeing the right of workers to organize themselves and to bargain and act collectively. In addition, the Labour Standards Law of 1947 provided standards for employment conditions such as working hours, safety regulations and minimum wages.

With such strong encouragement the Japanese labour movement experienced a phenomenal growth and expansion (up to 55.8 per cent organization rate in 1949). Until 1950 virtually all employees, including higher managerial levels, could be included in the union membership. Since then, only employees below the level of section chief can be a member as stipulated by law. From about 1950 onward, the organization rate started to drop, partly as a consequence of a reversal of policies which resulted in withdrawal of the right to strike from all civil servants, 'anti-communist' activities, etc.

Even though the labour movement had gained annually in *absolute* numbers, the rate of organization dropped beyond the one-third mark for the first time in 1973 (33.1%); then in 1974 and 1975 it improved somewhat (33.9 and 34.4% respectively) only to drop again to 33.7% in 1976 (12.5 million members).

While before the Second World War the labour organization seems to have been less successful in large firms than in small and medium ones, after the war the opposite became true; indeed the level of union enrolment is high in big enterprises and very low in small firms. One reason for the latter is the still quite feudalistic and paternalistic orientation of labour relations in many smaller enterprises, where it may be hard to organize a union, mainly because of emotional factors ('a revolt against the friendly atmosphere in the company family)'.

Large-scale corporations, on the other hand, might well be anxious to see that a union is formed within their organization, certainly if such a union is ready to collaborate with management to gain improvements in working conditions. Where labour-management harmony prevails management may regard union-management negotiations as a ready screening device of talented lower managerial employees; a sort of 'management-game training' where everybody knows the rules and the 'game' can be played accordingly. Not surprisingly, quite a few union leaders obtain substantial career improvements as soon as their term of office expires. Then large companies, many of them making huge profits and enjoying favourable credit facilities with banks and goodwill from the government, may easily attract union activity: such firms will be more likely to allow for considerable improvements in wages than will firms which have to struggle for their bare existence.

Taking all industries together, one will find that about one third of all eligible employees are actually members of a union. Most branches of manufacturing industry display approximately this same organization rate. In other sectors than manufacturing industries, one finds some very high rates (e.g. electricity, gas and water; public service; transport and communication, finance, insurance and real estate), or some rather low rates (service industries; construction; fishery and aquaculture; wholesale and retail).

The rate of organization is not the same for females and males. In recent years, less than 30 per cent of eligible females were organized, as compared with about 37-38 per cent of males. One possible explanation: many women are employed in agriculture, and in small family shops, where the rate of organization is very low. Furthermore, many females are employed on a part-time or temporary basis, and as such are not entitled to membership in the typical company union. (Contrastingly, a foreign manager repeatedly complained to me that in his company the female union members were much more 'venomous' than their male colleagues, who displayed a rather more obvious identification with management.)

The company union

Labour unions may be organized along several different lines. There are those that reach out nationally and cover several trades in which case one may speak of a national labour federation, while others limit their activities and interests to regional levels. Then there is the industrial union with members employed in a specific industry. Finally, there is what may be called the *company union* (company union may be called 'company-based union', 'enterprise union' or 'enterprise-based union' without any major distinction being intended): a union organization which accepts as its members only regular employees of a specific company or group of companies. The Japanese company union is very different from the local branch unit of a national, regional or industrial labour organization as existing in many other industrialized nations. Japanese company unions are basically autonomous, self-sufficient entities, operating independently within the confines of one clearly defined organization and within itself combining several trades and skill levels; it covers rank-and-file employees as well as lower level supervisory and managerial personnel.

The typical company union is involved in a broad range of activities. To name just a few: first it regularly confronts its management in collective bargaining sessions where except for normal issues (such as wages and related working conditions) all kinds of other matters may be formally brought up. Second, there is the highly important joint consultation through which a constant mutual flow of information is kept alive between management and labour. Third, many unions fulfill the role of a Mutual Aid Society for the benefit of their members and their relatives. Such activities may range from discount shops and loans, to holiday facilities.

The majority of union leaders at the company level are regular employees who may be temporarily relieved from other duties after having been elected to serve for their union. In principle they will be rewarded by the union as if they were still working while usually the company will give them the average bonus as paid to the whole work force. Among members of unions there is sometimes the suspicion that promotion considerations will easily influence a union leader's decisions: many top managers were once successful leaders of their company's union.

Japanese law prohibits companies from giving direct financial support to their union, but most major companies will render some indirect assistance like providing a meeting place, telephone, information board, and so on. The average union dues consist of about 1.5 per cent of average monthly regular earnings and thus will go up with any increase in wages or salaries. Enterprise unions may be very rich, having more financial resources than the national or industrial labour federation they belong to.

Labour solidarity among workers at the industry or national level has never been strong ; on the contrary the company's survival and prosperity ranks foremost for most company unions and solidarity even with non-regular employees working side by side with union members on the same shop floor has only rarely been displayed. On the other hand, while company unions will try to fight hard for their members' interests, they do not easily resort to drastic actions, preferring extended negotiations, token strikes or very short real strikes of a few days' maximum in order to accomplish their goals. Strikes are considered to be proof of bad management by the company and the union alike and thus, every means is taken to avert such overt action. Unions will be hesitant to initiate drastic campaigns for all sorts of reasons, not in the least because of the ever-present threat of the formation of a rival second union at management's instigation.

It would be incorrect to rigidly classify unions in the private sector as mere puppets but, essentially, the behaviour of many Japanese unions indeed seems to be governed to an important extent by the plight of their employers and by labour market conditions. During times of economic prosperity (as in the late 1960s and early 1970s) unions were able to make impressive gains throughout industry. From 1973, the recession progressively cut into their business, Japanese employers quickly reducing production and labour output. This was achieved through various means, starting with a cut back on overtime and on temporary workers and leading finally to paid lay-offs. Management stopped short, however, of dismissing any large portion of their regular work force. What happened then was a sharing of reduced incomes by employees in return for job security (as amply demonstrated during the spring wage negotiations of 1975-78).

Unions in the public sector

Japan's public sector is plagued with a great many conflicts between labour and management. One of the reasons undoubtedly is that while considerations of competition will often tend to moderate labour's demands in the private sector, such a restraining influence is lacking in the public sector where there is no competition. Many employees in the public sector are prohibited from striking and some from collective bargaining as well, while budgetary limitations (imposed by Parliament) render management rather powerless and put labour in a weak position as well: in such cases, disputes are mostly settled through compulsory arbitration. In recent years the *Shunto* (labour's spring offensive, see below) has brought the restoration of the right to strike in the centre of heated controversy. While workers in the relatively quiet private sector have a full guarantee of the right to strike and to bargain collectively, there is one category among these workers subjected to certain limitations: those who are employed in public utilities which are operated by private enterprises (an estimated 13% of organized labour employed, for example, in private railways). In such industries collective bargaining is relatively limited and parties may frequently be compelled to bargain at a national level, i.e. through special adjustment procedures involving mediation or arbitration by the Central Labour Relations Commission. (In the spring of 1977, management and labour in the private railway sector reached agreement on the 1977 wage increases without invoking such mediation: the first time in nine years.)

Labour Relations Commissions

National and local Labour Relations Commissions over the years have played an important role in Japan's labour relations system. They have often been called upon in situations where traditional methods of maintaining industrial peace threatened to fail. If possible such a commission will try to restrict itself to conciliation, an emotional appeal to both parties in order to reach a consensus. Only in stubborn cases formal mediation or arbitration may take place, but even then an appeal upon sentiments and mutual co-operative willingness will be preferred to a rational approach in which pros and cons are to be weighed by outsiders. (In April 1977, the Public Corporation and National Enterprise Labour Relations Commission went through this whole scale of activities before dictating its binding compromise to the government and unions concerned, notably those of the Japan National Railways.)[2]

There are many Labour Relations Commissions, each with specific areas of responsibility. The Central Labour Relations Commission is often called upon in conflicts between labour and management of important public utility industries. The Public Corporation and National Enterprise Labour Relations Commission is active in the embattled field of industrial relations where collective bargaining is allowed but striking is prohibited by law. Finally in this context the National Personnel Authority may be mentioned. Even though it is by no means a Labour Relations Commission, it is the institution to make recommendations to the government about remuneration, etc., of those employees who are legally prohibited from bargaining collectively or striking.

National Labour Federations

The Japanese company union being largely autonomous, by definition its entire existence tied up with that of its company, it is small
wonder that labour solidarity among workers at the industry or
national level has never really flourished (especially so in the private
sector). It is obvious that such an enterprise-unionism makes a
mixture of company and union interests quite probable. Union officials are subordinate to the very same managerial negotiators they
have to deal with at the bargaining table, where *direct* participation
from outside (e.g. officials of a national or industrial federation)
normally is not tolerated.

At present, around 90 per cent of Japanese unions (covering
about 80 per cent of organized labour) are organized on a company
basis. Over one third of the unionized labour force does *not* belong
to a labour federation at the *national* level but also unions which do
belong, remain quite independent. Similarly, if unions subscribe to
an organization at the *industry* level, their relation is quite loose and
allows for substantial independent action. About the only major
Japanese union which can be regarded as a national industrial
union in the usual Western conception is the All Japan Seamen's
Union.[3] There are in addition some *industrial* unions that have
taken over part of the member-unions' functions, e.g. private railway
workers, textile workers, coal mine workers and recently steel
workers, jointly negotiate wages and bonuses with employers'
associations (i.e. at the industry level), while leaving most other
matters to be decided at the respective bargaining tables of individual companies.

Thus it would be incorrect to say that higher level labour federations barely serve any purpose whatsoever: particularly since the
Shunto unionism (i.e. united labour action during spring time)
gained momentum at the national level from about 1960, whether or
not bargaining jointly at the industry level, organized labour has
become a factor not to be overlooked in Japan's socio-economic
pattern. In addition, many higher-level labour organizations provide
their own training programmes to be followed by members of their
respective member-unions. Still, enterprise unions are the main
representative of labour, negotiating mostly independently at company level with their management (maybe to obtain at least the
minimum gains suggested by their 'higher-level' national or industrial federation).

Many of the industry-level labour federations (themselves consisting of a number of enterprise unions in a certain branch of industry),
are constituting members of the national labour centres. The largest
national labour federation is *Sohyo* (General Council of Trade
Unions in Japan), almost exclusively representing organized labour
in the public sector, but also including substantial numbers in

private industry, leaning towards the left; second largest is *Domei* (Japanese Confederation of Labour) drawing the majority of its membership from the private sector and fostering a much more moderate policy towards management.

In June 1976 out of over 12.5 million unionists, almost 4.58 million belonged to a member union of Sohyo, almost 2.21 million to Domei, more than 1.35 million to Churitsuroren (Federation of Independent Unions) and about 66,000 to Shinsanbetsu (National Federation of Industrial Organizations). Almost 4.7 million unionists were members of unions which remained totally independent or subscribed to an independent industrial federation, such as the Confederation of Japanese Automobile Workers' Unions (Jidoshasoren, with about half a million members). Over 1.9 million Japanese unionists in 1975 were additionally affiliated to the International Metalworkers' Federation—Japan Council (IMF-JC), with which, for example, Jidoshasoren maintains contacts.[4]

In recent years mergers have often caused friction within enterprise unions, particularly if the two companies have unions belonging one to Sohyo and one to Domei. A few mergers have actually failed because of union resistance. Domei has been the one to gain most through mergers or other business combinations: the moderate, more co-operative line naturally was favoured by the managements involved.

Sohyo explicitly supports the Japan Socialist Party, and Domei the left-of-centre Democratic Socialist Party. The very strong attachment between the political opposition and the national labour centres, notably Sohyo, has led to frequent accusations that industrial disputes are used exclusively for political purposes.[5] Taira suggests that the Japanese labour movement has no other recourse but to side with the political opposition, because the Japanese government has consistently refused to treat labour as a worthy socio-economic partner and as a force to be consulted on policy matters. He says that while 'the "habit of mutual consultation" exists between business and the government on all socio-economic problems, the extreme difficulty that ... besets the labour movement when it wants to make its voice heard directly by the representatives of the government takes on an air of scandalous nepotism by the political standards of participatory democracies of the West.'[6] The three main opposition parties (i.e. the Communist, the Socialist and the Democratic Socialist Parties) depend heavily upon organized labour for their essential support. Historically speaking, Japanese labour and political opposition were closely intertwined: already in the earliest years of this century, the only way for organized labour to operate was through official political parties (however limited), since oppressive legislation made virtually all other action totally impossible. Then, as some time after the Second

World War most of labour's fundamental rights were taken away from labour in the public sector, once more the only way left to press for improvements in labour conditions was through semi-political pressure.

Employers organizations

Even though employers' organizations traditionally have wielded substantially more power at the national level than has organized labour, it is incumbent upon the management team at each individual company to confront labour over the bargaining table and reach agreement there. Employers' organizations will, however, issue non-binding guidelines well before the yearly spring round of negotiations; their function thus becomes that of 'battlecrier' or 'scapegoat', to be used as handy excuses for a tough stand.

Employers are organized on an industrial, regional and/or national basis. *Keidanren* (Federation of Economic Organizations) is the most powerful association, combining in itself a substantial number of major firms and industrial, trade and financial associations. It aims at studying important economic problems, giving advice or suggestions to the government on economic policies and assisting in implementing them. The *Nissho* (Chamber of Commerce and Industry) represents a great many medium and small scale firms through a large network of chambers of commerce and industry all over Japan. *Keizai Doyukai* (Committee for Economic Development) originally recruited its membership from among younger industrialists, bankers, etc, whose major intention was to scrutinize existing management practices and to formulate alternative policies. *Nikkeiren* (Federation of Employers' Associations) is the major spokesman for management at large in confrontation with organized labour. There is no denying that employers' political influence is very considerable and so far has had the most pervasive impact on the national government in economic and general policy matters.

In recent years, a number of union federations at industrial level (textile workers, coal miners, steel workers) have taken on the responsibility of negotiating wage matters on behalf of their member unions, with their respective employers' organizations. In this way managements of individual companies had to give up part of their independence as well; however, since employers had a much longer tradition of co-operation than had unions, this did not seem to cause any major problems.

Shunto (Labour's Spring Offensive)

While soon after the War a pattern evolved of union-management negotiations at the company level only, an increasing need was being felt to unite labour in an effort to be stronger against management (that was already relatively well united on national and regional levels). Particularly in the public sector and in some branches of private industry where productivity tended to lag behind, labour got aware of the desirability of more or less joint action. Thus it was *Sohyo* which together with *Churitsuroren* (Federation of Independent Unions) took the initiative for the *Shunto* to take place, in 1955 (spring labour offensive : *shun* = spring, and *to* = struggle).

Not only was the advantage of scale one of the considerations, joint action was also intended to help the powerless public-sector labour gain about the same improvements as its counterpart in the private sector. The beginnings were only moderate, no more than 730,000 workers (11.7 per cent of organized labour and 4.2 per cent of all employees) being involved as of 1955. But their number increased very rapidly. Shunto came to be looked upon as a viable means for labour to present itself as one front, be it with preservation of the basic enterprise union structure. For the 1976 Shunto an estimate held that about 9 million unionists were somehow involved, about a quarter of all employees.

Domei (traditionally Sohyo's number one rival with a strong foothold in the private sector) initially did not take part in the yearly spring offensive. But Shunto made such great strides forward, that during the 1960s Domei-affiliated unions or union federations started joining in, either directly, or indirectly through co-ordinated timing schedules, etc. Domei still largely follows a hands-off policy, but provides guidelines to its affiliates taking part.

Over the years, Sohyo-originated demands have tended to be of the very high 'minimum demand' type, while Domei put more stress on moderate and 'realistic' targets. Shunto preparations start as early as August or September of the preceding year. The 'joint spring offensive committee' usually chaired by the top man of Sohyo draws up a list of demands to be presented in next year's spring and publishes these in a White Paper. Once the targets have been formulated the committee selects *pattern setters* which are the ones to start the major wave of co-ordinated negotiations early in the next spring. Then, long before the due date, many an industrial federation announces, along with its minimum demands, a schedule of strikes which are to be staged, specially in the public sector. Some time in March, the first negotiations usually take place. Results are widely publicized and other unions use the results of previous negotiations to press for similar concessions from their own management. It should be stressed that most of the strikes take place in the public sector (if at all) having a direct impact on the nation's daily life.

From its outset (1955) until its virtual climax in 1974, Shunto developments displayed a distinct pattern. While initially one of the stated aims was to give support to unions in the public sector, in the early 1970s the issue of strike rights for employees in the public sector had become a major point of contention and conflict; Shunto had become very much radicalized, with bitter strike tactics evoking retaliation from authorities concerned, etc, etc. This climax also coincided with the era of phenomenally high economic growth, when labour succeeded in obtaining large wage increases: 18.5 per cent in 1970; 16.9 per cent in 1971; 15.3 per cent in 1972; 20.1 per cent in 1973; 32.9 per cent in inflation-plagued 1974[7] (it was 13.1%, 8.8% and about 9% in 1975, 1976, 1977).

In 1974, the government promised to study the right of strike issue. This was also the year that the aftermath of 1973s oil crisis was most seriously felt. From the 1975 Shunto on, then, one observes a different 'mood' in the annual confrontations, with more moderate union federations taking the lead. The 1977 Shunto thus showed a pattern which may become typical for the Japanese labour-relations scene under conditions of low economic growth. For one thing, it seems that the highly militant posture of some unions in the public sector (which terrorized Japan in the early 1970s, and became highly unpopular with the general public) will lose its impact, both because of dislike among the public and more objective socio-economic variables.[8]

The 1977 spring labour offensive, then, evolved as follows. After extensive negotiations from about early March, four industrial union federations in the metal-related industries were offered wage increases in mid-April, thus confirming their role of pattern setters in the Shunto process (like before). All four federations are members of the International Metalworkers' Federation—Japan Council (IMF-JC). While business results and prospects were great for the electrical equipment and appliances, as well as for the automobile industries, the situation looked less favourable for the steel and ship-building sectors. Labour's strategy of linking up these four branches resulted in slightly higher wage raise proposals for the electrical appliances (9.50 per cent) and automobiles (9.99 per cent) branches—though actually lower than one might have anticipated—and slightly lower wage raise proposals for the steel sector (8.54 per cent) and ship-building (8.67 per cent)—though actually higher than one might have anticipated. The proposals were accepted. Thus a significant pattern had been set: the inflation rate had run at about 9.2 per cent, and the willingness of unions in prosperous sectors to moderate and tie their demands to those from the depressed sectors produced generally acceptable results.

Next were the private railways (as usual among the first again) where the unions in the early 1970s had readily joined in with those in the public sector, calling strikes and slow-downs well before any formal negotiations had taken place. Now, for the first time in nine years and after extensive preliminary negotiations, the 'negotiate first then strike' principle was maintained; and no assistance was requested from the Central Labour Relations Commission. The unions accepted a 9.1 per cent wage increase offer, and management added a one-time payment of 30,000 yen per worker, as if to encourage labour to continue the newly-founded more peaceful approach. After all this, unions in the public sector (already appalled by negative reactions about their strike convulsions in previous years) could not but take a quiet line as well: without more than token tactics, they accepted a compromise proposal from the Public Corporation and National Enterprise Labour Relations Commission: a 9.12 per cent raise.

Thus it seems that the call for moderation (embodied in the majority of private industry labour organizations, even during the earlier years of enormous economic expansion) had finally gained an upper hand over the more militancy-prone advocacy as was typical for unions in the public sector. Both (anticipated) labour market forces and the likelihood that most workers in the public sector will be granted some form of right to strike (as hinted by the government in 1974) will have contributed to this outcome. It is likely that the near future will see similar patterns, rather than a retreat to the same militant tactics that characterized the early 1970s.

What next

There is no denying that since the beginning of Shunto working hours have been reduced considerably and wages have gone up tremendously. Even though successive governments have been inclined to neglect organized labour, the urge from management to involve labour in major national policy decisions is increasingly being heard. Employers also have been forced to formulate clear policy lines at the national, industrial and company level; at the same time, union leaders have gained considerably in negotiating skill and power.

Finally, Shunto has played a role in the development towards some form of joint play between unions at national level and towards a gradual diminishing of the parochialism that was characteristic of Japanese unionism for a long time.

Shunto developments undeniably have been a step away from the isolationist tendencies inherent in company unionism. This should not be overrated though, the company union is still the major actor in the confrontation of Japanese labour and management. Recent years, moreover, have demonstrated a clear tendency for *Sohyo* to represent the public sector and *Domei* the private sector, as two separate and diverse spheres of action.

Proposals regarding the formation of one united labour front in Japan have been repeatedly made. The reasoning was obvious: while employers were united in solid organizations, employees still were divided over rival federations that adhered to basically different ideologies. Some years ago, before the 1973 oil crisis, a proposal originated from the minority private-industry sector within *Sohyo*, which was eagerly accepted by *Domei*. Experts, however, saw the possibility of an even sharper division between labour of the private and public sector: *Sohyo's* member unions in the *private* sector had already repeatedly shown some degree of aversion from the militant stand taken by unions in the public sector. Leadership of *Sohyo* and *Domei*, even though in principle agreeing to the desirability of labour unity, never have been really able to bridge the existing fundamental differences in ideology.

One point deserving special attention lies in the likelihood that employees in the public sector will soon be granted some right to strike. *Sohyo* has long been able to gather support around this very issue. One may wonder whether the absence of this struggle point, in addition to the rather slow economic growth to be expected, will not result in considerable alienation of many unions from the radical line, once the recognition of labour's fundamental rights would have brought relative peace and quiet to the public sector as well.

One can only guess about further developments. It would not be too surprising if increased attention was given to unionization of labour in small enterprises and among underprivileged labour groups in general, i.e. those sectors of the working population that have so far been largely neglected by Japan's official labour movement. One of the probable results would be an increased emphasis on unionization at the regional or industrial level. In the future, one might even find a picture like this: one major labour federation combining unions of employees in larger firms (based on the principle of enterprise unionism) and another major federation concentrating on other, less privileged, groups within the working population, notably organizing workers at the industrial or regional level. Such a development would basically maintain similar divisions as those that exist within Japanese labour at present, destroying hopes for a unity of labour in the foreseeable future.

1. After a number of court rulings (notably in 1966 and 1969) favouring a relatively lenient treatment of unionists who acted against the law (prohibiting strikes for employees in the public sector), in May 1977 the Supreme Court suddenly reversed this trend, thus opening the way for tougher law-enforcement.

2. In April 1978 there was even a distinct impression that the same unions (hard pressed to 'face realities') actually welcomed official mediation procedures as a public face-saving manipulation to accept an exceptionally low average pay rise of 5.4 per cent.

3. This union gained international attention during its prolonged, indeed 'un-Japanese' strike, early 1972.

4. *Yearbook of labour statistics, 1976* (Tokyo: Ministry of Labour, 1977), 346-349.

5. Dealing with the conflict between labour and management in Japan's public sector, the governing body of the International Labour Organization in 1973 accepted a report concluding 'that the principles of freedom of association do not apply for the organization of strikes for purely political objectives and strikes which are systematically scheduled long before negotiations even begin to take place.' However, during the early 1970s this sort of strikes were a yearly recurring phenomenon in Japan's public sector, to the inconvenience of millions of commuters, etc.

6. Taira K. *Economic development and the labour market in Japan* (New York and London: Columbia University Press, 1970), p 234.

7. From 1955 there was a positive correlation between the rate of wage raises and the supply-demand ratio in the job market (with the exception of 1974 only). A number of studies have reached the same conclusion: it was not so much the unions' bargaining power, as labour market forces which were influential in determining wage rises. Other factors of importance were company profits and consumer price raises, in that order. See: *Japan Labour Bull,* Dec 1974, 5-8; Taira K. *Economic development and the labor market in Japan* (New York: Columbia University Press, 1970), 198-202.

8. In spite of all outward appearances, it was obvious during 1978's Spring Labour Offensive that the era of 'low economic growth' had been accepted as an irreversible fact. This is aptly reflected in following quote from *Nihon Keizai Shimbun's* (English edition of 2 May, 1978: 'For Japanese workers, drastic wage level increases (such as 25-30 per cent gains now enjoyed by South Korean workers) are already things of the past. From now on, the sizes of wage level increases will work as excellent indicators of the vitality of the Japanese economy as a whole. As far as this year's wage hikes are concerned, it is clear that the Japanese economy is largely devoid of the vigour which once made it famous'. (The meagre outcome of the 1978 Shunto to some observers even signalled the gradual demise of the 'Spring Offensive' itself.)

Appendix 1

The Employees' Pension Insurance roughly covers all employees of companies in which five or more persons are normally employed. All these employees are compulsorily insured, while other persons may be covered voluntarily. In March 1976 almost 23.6 million employees were insured, including almost 1.5 million on a voluntary basis. Most male employees under this scheme pay 9.1 per cent (1978) of their monthly standard remuneration as a premium, which is shared in equal proportion between employer and employee; (the rate in 1972 was 7.6 per cent). Most female employees pay 7.3 per cent (1978) (the rate for 1972 was 5.8 per cent). The benefits include an *annual amount* to be paid to those who have been insured for at least 20 years *and* who have reached the age of 60, provided that they are not employed any more (in most cases). This *annual amount* is made up of a *basic amount* and an *additional* one. The *basic amount* consists of a flat rate of ¥1650 multiplied by the number of months paid up (with a minimum of 240 months and a maximum of 420 months' equivalent), and an amount proportionate to the average monthly standard remuneration of the insured (this sum is equal to 1 per cent of the average monthly standard remuneration multiplied by the number of months paid up). The *additional amount* is granted for dependants (¥72,000 for a supported spouse; ¥24,000 for the first and second children under 18, and ¥4,800 for each additional child). There are several other benefits, including survivor's pension and invalidity pension.

In 1974 a sliding-scale system was introduced through which the pension is adjusted as soon as the price index has risen by 5 per cent. As of October 1976, the average monthly amount received under this scheme was ¥68,000, still quite low, but far better than some years ago. In addition, there is a considerable number of people who do not fulfil the minimum requirement of 20 years and therefore are not entitled to receive normal benefits under this scheme (though some minor changes were recently initiated). In fact, in November 1970 there were a great many elderly people who, for some reason or other, did not receive any public old-age pension, as may be seen from Table 1.

140

Table 1

PERCENTAGE OF PEOPLE RECEIVING PUBLIC OLD-AGE PENSION BY AGE
GROUPS (1970)

Age	Total	Total of recipients	Monthly pension less than ¥10,000	¥10,000-¥20,000	over ¥20,000	Total percentage of non-recipients
Total	100.0%	15.8%	1.7%	9.9%	4.2%	84.2%
-58	100.0	5.2	0.5	1.4	3.3	94.8
59-60	100.0	21.6	2.3	13.6	5.7	78.4
61-62	100.0	35.5	1.6	28.9	5.0	64.5
63-64	100.0	35.9	2.4	23.5	10.0	65.1
65-	100.0	73.1	24.4	43.1	5.6	26.8

Source: Survey on people reaching retirement age. In *White paper on national life, 1973—the life and its quality in Japan* (Tokyo: Economic Planning Agency, Japanese Government, 1973), 81.

These figures represented a harsh reality, which in spite of some recent indications of (impending) improvements have not been modified to any substantial degree; on the contrary, the tremendous inflation of recent years has practically wiped out subsequent improvements.

While the old-age pension under the Employees' Pension Insurance is not really impressive, the other two main public pension schemes provide even less security, in spite of recent modifications.

The Contributory National Pension. Japanese residents between 20 and 59 are compulsorily insured under this scheme, provided that those covered under one of the other public pension schemes, the beneficiaries of other pension schemes, spouses of these two groups and students are excluded from coverage. Latter groups shall be covered voluntarily. In 1976, almost 26 million persons were insured under this scheme, 5.8 million on a voluntary basis. At the same time there were over 2.7 million beneficiaries of old age pension to whom almost ¥460 billion was paid out. Most people pay ¥2,200 monthly. The benefits include an amount to be paid to those who have been insured for at least 25 years (with some exceptions; like under the previous scheme a 'co-ordinated old-age pension' was recently established to bridge some existing gaps in the system). In addition, the insured may be entitled to receive an invalidity pension, widowed mother's pension, and other benefits. However, the amounts disbursed remain scant, far below subsistence level needs.

The Non-contributory National Pension covers roughly those people who for some reason are not entitled to contributory pension payments, including those who were exempted from insurance contributions because of their low income. In March 1976, there were almost 5.14 million beneficiaries who received some kind of benefits under this scheme (in total ¥706 billion was paid out). Benefits included: old-age pension, invalidity pension, widowed mother's pension, and guardian's pension. However, the amounts disbursed remain at a pitifully low level.

Appendix 2

Generalized schematic representation of career possibilities under the shikaku seido
(Regular Employees)

Junior high-school graduates' starting point (age 15)

Senior high-school graduates' starting point (age 18)

Higher education (age 20-22) graduates' starting point

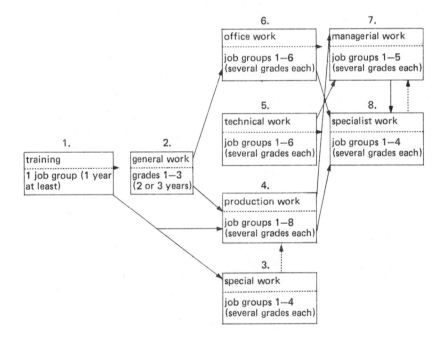

Note 1 : Stages 1 and 2 may be combined and/or shortened, depending on technical requirements of the production process.

Note 2 : Blocks 3 through 8 represent the broad job categories existing under the *shikaku seido*.

Note 3 : Each of the job categories consists of several job groups (whose number may vary per company, but often will largely coincide with the figures given here) ; in turn, every job group consists of a number of job grades, corresponding to subtle differences in wages and salaries.

The following paragraphs contain some additional remarks about most of the eight blocks in the figure; these descriptions may provide additional insight into the workings of the *shikaku seido,* for each of the three employee types (with junior high school, senior high school, or higher education, respectively).

Block 1. Where junior high-school graduates are admitted, they usually form one job-group for at least one year, during which period they receive some fundamental training, mainly through on-the-job instruction. This group is often called *minarai,* which means look-learn. The 'trainee category' has no further subgroups and is mostly represented by one specific job grade. Their remuneration is often based on their age, like in the case of Matsushita where for the employees aged 15 to 17 a minimum rate has been fixed for each age group.

The promotion chances of this group are slim, even though in theory the way may be open to them to reach managerial ranks by means of successive training and education courses and superior performance. Yet it is very rare for any one in this group to reach the position of supervisor. Most of them after some years, are classified in the lowest job group of the production work category and then their career consists of step-by-step (almost automatic) advancements through successive job grades and job groups within the same category. By the time of reaching the age limit, most of them will have entered the upper reaches of the highest job group, i.e. just below the lowest managerial level. If an employee reaches the top of the non-supervisory ladder some years before his retirement, he may be promoted into the category of 'specialists'. A minority of the junior high-school leavers may be classified in the job category of 'special work', i.e. security man or driver.

Block 2. Senior high school leavers usually start at the level of *ippan shoku* (general work), which may also be the intermediate category for junior high-school leavers before they are classified into any one of the real job categories (production, office or technical). A young employee may remain in this 'general work' category for about two or three years, during which a variety of fundamental training courses is to be followed. This *ippan shoku* category often consists of about three grades, and in most cases a minimum wage is fixed according to age. Employees in this category will be classified into the 'production work' category, while others will be assigned to low-level office work or technical work. Even though promotion into the lowest supervisory ranks is the final target of many production employees, the actual scope of such positions is limited since there are many low-level supervisor positions.

The career chances for senior high-school leavers are relatively limited in so far that only a few of them ever reach supervisory ranks before retirement. Real promotion in this group seems to be based more upon ability than is the case among university graduates.

Block 3. The 'special work' category should not be confused with the 'specialist' category (block 8). In this category are included porters, drivers, cleaning women, telephone operators, gardeners. There are no real prospects of advancement for these employees, except for yearly increments of status and remuneration. Only in rare cases some improvement might be gained through reclassification into the production job category at a relatively early age.

Blocks 4, 5, 6 and 7. While high-school leavers enter one of these categories after some years of preparation, college and university graduates are immediately classified in one of these real job categories (production, technical or office work) and frequently in the third job group or so. It should be mentioned that university graduates may rotate between production, technical and office-work categories in the course of their career. For many of them such rotations are part of their training schedule. Lower level employees usually stay within the main work category once they have been classified at the beginning of their career.

Block 8. The 'specialist' category is often used to 'promote' less successful managers into areas where they can function relatively well but without major responsibilities. In recent years many firms have felt the necessity to employ outside experts in specific fields such as computer science and systems engineering: they are included in this category.

Very promising people may also join the rank of the 'specialists' on a strictly temporary basis until an appropriate place is found for them somewhere else in the organization. The 'specialists' salary is not too different from that of their more fortunate colleagues who hold real position and have subordinates under their command, but it is usual for the real manager to receive substantially larger bonuses and allowances to reward him for his superior performance.

Appendix 3

The composition of monthly earnings

There are a great many different wage and salary systems in operation in Japanese industry. They all seem to have in common that they consist of a substantial proportion of *standard pay,* including the *basic salary* (which in turn usually consists of some kind of *basic pay* and some other *main components),* and a variety of *allowances,* plus a smaller proportion of *extra pay,* which may include overtime and similar payments. The great diversity is to be found mainly in the composition of the standard pay, especially since in recent years many firms have started to emphasize the kind of work and to some extent, the quality of work performance for particular groups of employees.

The definition of *basic salary* (basis for so many other payments) differs from one company to the other, but usually it consists of one or two components which are almost exclusively based upon previous education, sex and seniority, maybe complemented with a few components which tend to reflect kind of work and quality of performance (Table 1).

Salary composition of 'Company X'

In order to clarify this whole complicated matter at least to a certain degree, I present the example of the salary composition as utilized in a major manufacturing firm in 1972. The data in table 1 concern only male regular employees of this company who are union members (i.e., below the level of section chief). It may also be noted in advance that in this particular company no junior high-school graduates are hired, so that senior high-school graduates are to be found in production and maintenance as well as in staff areas. University graduates here are exclusively classified as staff. The right-hand column gives a characterization of the pay elements concerned, as provided by the company itself. I have chosen this particular example because I consider it to be representative of the main-stream of salary-composition practices in the most important sectors of Japanese industry.

Table 1

SALARY COMPOSITION IN COMPANY X FOR MALE REGULAR EMPLOYEES UNION MEMBERS, 1972

	Staff yen amount	%	P & M employees yen amount	%	Determining factors for pay level per type of employee
Basic pay	40,622	(46.9)	37,870	(44.0)	Personal factors like age, length of service, academic career and experience; for all employees.
Pay for job and ability	44,104	(51.0)	—		Job performance, judged ability, qualification and contribution; for staff only (white collars, also including foremen).
Pay for job	—		19,665	(22.9)	Degree of difficulty and importance of job and working conditions, eg, as determined by job evaluation; for P & M only (blue collars).
Additional pay for job	—		5,198	(6.0)	Individual differences in performance on the same job; for P & M only (blue collars).
Efficiency pay (group premium)	—		11,768	(13.6)	Efficiency of each shop (by output, manhours spent, time needed); for P & M only (blue collars).
Adjustment pay	—		6,604	(7.7)	A payment resulting from recent developments, including a merger. This is temporary; P & M only (blue collars).
Various allowances	1,859	(2.1)	4,885	(5.7)	(for descriptions: see further on)
Standard pay TOTAL	86,585	(100.0)	85,990	(100.0)	
Overtime allowance	13,288	(15.3)	6,235	(7.2)	(see further on)
Night duty	803	(0.9)	5,177	(6.0)	
Extra pay TOTAL	14,091	(16.2)	11,412	(13.2)	
TOTAL	100,676	(116.2)	97,402	(113.2)	(=total average cash earnings)

(STANDARD PAY applies to Basic pay through Standard pay TOTAL rows; Extra pay applies to Overtime allowance and Night duty rows.)

Basic salary: the main components

The *basic salary* in most companies includes some distinct *main components*. In the present example, blue-collar production-and-maintenance workers' basic salary includes five of such components. White collars' basic salary consists of only two main components.

White-collar staff. The basic salary of white-collar personnel in Company X consists of the 'basic pay' and the 'pay for job and ability' components. The characterizations as given in Table 1 right-hand column reveal that apparently personal factors like age, length of service, academic career and experience, along with judged ability, qualification and contribution are the important determinants of the average monthly salary. An incidental mentioning of 'job performance' completes the description of those factors which are of greatest relevance in the salary determination of white collars.

Blue-collar employees. Almost half (44 per cent) of the blue collar's basic salary consists of the *basic pay* which is based upon strictly personal, not directly work-related factors. The blue-collar employee's earnings are determined by kind of work and performance to a slightly higher extent when compared with white collars. *Pay for job* is related to job-evaluation results. It is through this pay for job that the kind of work performed (at the blue-collar level) has an impact upon the average earnings. In the above example this component covers about 23 per cent of the total standard pay, while recent developments clearly indicate that (for blue collars) the kind-of-work component is gaining importance. On the other hand, the *efficiency pay* (in most firms a group incentive) has gradually lost influence in recent years. This efficiency pay relates only indirectly to the individual's efforts, by definition. The only component of the standard pay depending directly upon individual differences in performance is the minor *additional pay for job.*

Adjustment source. Table 1 indicates that blue collars have a slightly greater chance to influence their earnings (through the work they perform and the quality of their performance) than white collars. The wage of production and maintenance workers 'tends to become higher as it involves more elements for growth', according to X Company's information. That's why this company (like many others) operates an *adjustment source.* The idea of this system is to make *pay for the job and ability* of staff employees correspond to the *pay for job, additional pay for job, efficiency pay* and *adjustment pay* of P & M workers. The total amounts paid per head of both types of employees during the past six months are obtained semi-annually according to a fixed rule. The excess of the total amount per head for P & M workers over that for staff employees is reserved as the adjustment source, which is supplied to staff employees at the time of bonus payment.

This explains why white collars usually obtain much higher bonus amounts than blue collars. One may conclude that, in cases like these, white collars' *bonuses* strongly depend upon the work of blue collars, surely not only on their own!

A variety of allowances

Within the large variety of allowances which may complement the basic salary, a major distinction is to be made between *duty allowances* and *cost-of-living allowances.* In total, i.e., proportionate to the average monthly contractual earnings minus overtime, duty allowances accounted for 4.1 per cent and living-cost allowances for 6.6 per cent of those monthly earnings in 1973. Both percentages have shown a steady increase over recent years. Duty allowances are relatively more important in smaller firms, living-cost allowances clearly so in larger firms.

An important duty allowance is the *position allowance* or *supervisory allowance.* Those who perform managerial or supervisory duties receive an allowance instead of extra basic salary. This is done in order to keep the seniority-based automatic progression of the basic salary intact, particularly in view of the fact that retirement allowances, bonuses and similar payments are based on the basic salary. Table 2 reveals interesting differences between small and large firms.

Table 2

MONTHLY POSITION AND SUPERVISORY ALLOWANCES
VARIOUS COMPANY SIZES, OSAKA, 1973 (in yen and (%))

Position	All companies	1000+ employees	300-999 employees	100-299 employees	99 or less employees
Department Head	26,393 yen (=100.0%)	32,819 yen (=100.0)	24,954 yen (=76.0)	27,000 yen (=82.3)	24,397 yen (=74.3)
Section Chief	15,723 yen (=59.6)	19,764 yen (=100.0)	15,768 yen (=79.8)	16,114 yen (=81.5)	14,232 yen (=72.0)
Assistant Manager	6,072 yen (=23.0)	5,808 yen (=100.0)	5,609 yen (=96.6)	6,259 yen (=107.8)	6,248 yen (=107.6)
Supervisor	12,368 yen (=100.0)	4,381 yen (=100.0)	11,707 yen (=267.2)	12,370 yen (=282.4)	14,266 yen (=325.6)
Foreman	6,585 yen (=53.2)	2,825 yen (=100.0)	5,630 yen (=199.3)	7,933 yen (=280.8)	7,021 yen (=248.5)
Group Leader	2,205 yen (=17.8)	850 yen (=100.0)	1,309 yen (=154.0)	1,971 yen (=213.9)	3,092 yen (=363.8)

Source: *1973 model wages for non-graduate recruitees in Osaka* (Osaka: Chamber of Commerce and Industry, 1974), p. 7.

The comparison of allowances in companies of different sizes reveals the familiar pattern only for higher managerial ranks: there bigger firms pay more, but lower in the hierarchy, and at the production level anyway, smaller firms tend to pay more than bigger ones. Probably this is related to the fact that the seniority principle is not very consistently practised in small firms, so that responsibility is to be rewarded directly. In big companies higher responsibility at least partially is an automatic consequence of higher seniority which in turn is reflected in higher pay anyway.

The Labour Ministry defines the *allowance for specific working conditions* as 'the allowance paid for specific working conditions, different from standard conditions, or for specific jobs, different from normal' while the *allowance for specific services* is described as 'the allowance paid for specified service different from the normal'. In 1973 these two allowances together accounted for almost 1.5 per cent of the average standard pay.

Employees involved in shift work receive a *shift allowance* and employees receive a *night-duty allowance* for work performed between 10 pm and 5 am. Night-duty allowances are often considered to be part of the *extra pay* component of monthly earnings rather than part of the *standard pay.*

Among cost-of-living allowances, the most important is the *family allowance* which is related to the number of dependents of the employee. Table 3 leaves no doubt as to the relation between company size and amounts of family allowance paid.

Table 3

AVERAGE PAYMENT OF FAMILY ALLOWANCE BY COMPANY SIZE (in yen)

	1000 or more employees	100-999 employees	30-99 employees
1st dependant	3,633 yen	2,240 yen	1,855 yen
2nd dependant	1,166 yen	884 yen	851 yen
3rd dependant	1,049 yen	744 yen	743 yen
4th dependant	931 yen	701 yen	732 yen

Source: *Yearbook of labour statistics, 1972* (Tokyo: Ministry of Labour, 1973), p.189.

In 1973 a *housing allowance* was paid in 71 per cent of companies surveyed by the Ministry of Labour to employees who did not occupy any company housing (house, flat or dormitory). Depending on marital status and family responsibility and also on the kind of housing an employee is living in, the amount of housing allowance may vary substantially within one company.

In 1972 almost 90 per cent of sampled companies paid a *commuting allowance* to their personnel to compensate for the expenses incurred when travelling to and from their work.

A *regional allowance* is paid in some cases: companies with head office in Tokyo or Osaka pay a special amount to their employees of those head offices, but not to employees of their production plants located in the countryside where prices are much lower.

In order to encourage good attendance some companies pay extra cash for a full or nearly full attendance record: the *attendance allowance.*

Extra pay (mainly overtime pay)

All these allowances, in addition to the basic pay (with its main components), constitute together the *standard pay,* to which must now be added the *extra pay* which consists almost completely of *overtime pay* (though *night duty* allowances are often included in this extra pay).

Normally overtime allowances are paid to employees below the managerial rank of section chief. Those who are not entitled to receive overtime pay are commonly compensated by means of other allowances (position allowance, responsibility allowance, etc.).

A Ministry of Labour survey (conducted in September 1973) in a very large sample of enterprises with at least 30 employees, revealed that overtime allowances accounted for almost 11 per cent of total monthly cash earnings. In large companies (with 1,000 or more employees) this percentage was 12.8, in medium-sized and small firms 10.0 and 8.2 respectively. (In the aftermath of the Oil Crisis of the same year, managements all over cut back on overtime work; while the prevailing criticism till then had been that workers were forced to work far too many hours, now the main complaint became that workers were earning substantially less, because of reductions in overtime work).

(Note: no extra mention is made here of seasonal allowances, or bonuses and retirement allowances which by some are regarded as inherent parts of an employee's monthly earnings.)

Appendix 4

To give an impression about what kind of punishment may be applied for what sort of misconduct, the following excerpt of a shipbuilding firm's disciplinary regulations for blue-collar employees may be helpful.

Light punishment (not including discharge) may be incurred by employees, for instance if they:
—obstruct others in carrying out their duty
—create disorder on the company's premises
—use company property for private purposes
—cause accidents by obvious neglect
—fight or quarrel within the company's premises
—punch the clock for someone else, or have this done for themselves
—plaster walls or paste posters without permission
—modify official company information (information boards, etc.)

Heavy punishment (including discharge) may be incurred by employees, for instance if they:
—leave the workplace frequently and for long periods, without permission or proper reason
—without proper reason neglect orders given by a superior or other person in charge
—neglect safety or hygiene regulations
—at application time, falsify data in their personal history
—perform work at another company, without permission
—release information to the company's detriment, or disclose work-related secrets
—spend company funds dishonestly, steal, or physically damage company products or property
—without permission arrange meetings, discussions, fund raisings, on the company's premises
—without permission carry badges or head-bands for political or propaganda purposes, on the company's premises
—after due process, have been classified as criminal according to penal law (including police arrests).

Selected bibliography:

1. Abegglen, J. C. ed. *Business strategies for Japan* (Tokyo: Brittanica/Sophia University), 1970.
2. —*Management and worker: the Japanese solution* (Tokyo-New York: Sophia University/Kodansha Int. Ltd.), 1973.
3. Adams, T. F. M. and Kobayashi N. *The world of Japanese business—an authoritative analysis* (Tokyo, etc.: Kodansha International Ltd.), 1974 (4th printing).
4. Allen, G. D. *A short economic history of modern Japan* (New York: Praeger Publishers, rev. ed.), 1963.
5. —*Japan's economic recovery* (New York: Oxford University Press), 1958.
6. Arai, S. *An intersection of East and West: Japanese business management* (Tokyo: Rikugei Publishing House), 1971.
7. Ayusawa, I. F. *A history of labor in modern Japan* (Honolulu: East-West Center Press), 1966.
8. Ballon, R. J. ed. *The Japanese employee* (Tokyo: Sophia University/Tuttle), 1969.
9. —*Doing business in Japan* (Tokyo: Sophia University/Tuttle, 3rd ed.), 1970.
10. Barnlund, D. C. The public self and private self in Japan and the United States. In Condon J. C. and Saito, M. eds. *Intercultural encounters with Japan* (Tokyo: the Simul Press), 1974.
11. Beardsley, R. K. *Studies in Japanese culture* (Ann Arbor: University of Michigan Press), 1965.
12. Ben Dasan I. (pseud.): *The Japanese and the Jews* (New York-Tokyo: Weatherhill), 1972.
13. Bendix, D. A case study in cultural and educational mobility: Japan and the protestant ethic. In Smelser N. and Lipset, S. eds. *Social structure and mobility in economic development* (Chicago: Aldine Publishing Co.), 1966.
14. Benedict, R. *The chrysanthemum and the sword* (Boston: Houghton-Mifflin), 1946.
15. Bennett, J. W. and Ishino I. *Paternalism in the Japanese economy: anthropological studies of oyabun-kobun patterns* (Minneapolis: University of Minnesota Press), 1963.
16. Boxer, C. R. *The Dutch seaborne empire: 1600-1800* (London: Hutchinson), 1965.
17. —*Jan Compagnie in Japan: 1600-1817* (Tokyo-London etc.: Oxford University Press), 1968.
18. Caudill W. and Scarr, H.A., Japanese value orientations and culture change. In Lebra T. S. and Lebra W. P. eds. *Japanese culture and behavior: selected readings* (Honolulu: University Press of Hawaii), 1974.
19. Cole, R. E. *Japanese blue collar: the changing tradition* (Berkeley-Los Angeles, London: University of California Press),1971.
20. Condon, J. C., Introduction: a perspective for the conference. In: Condon, J. C. and Saito M. *Intercultural encounters with Japan* (Tokyo: the Simul Press), 1974.
21. Craig, A. M. and Shively, D. H. eds. *Personality in Japanese History* (Berkeley: University of California Press), 1970.
22. Creemers, W. H. M. *Shrine Shinto after World War II* (Leiden, Holland: Brill), 1968.
23. De Vos G., and Wagatsuma, H. *Japan's invisible race: caste in culture and personality* (Berkeley: University of California Press), 1966.
24. De Vos, G. A., *Socialization for achievement: essays on the cultural psychology of the Japanese* (Berkeley: University of California Press), 1973 (with contributions by H. Wagatsuma, W. Caudill and K. Mizushima).

156

25. De Menthe, B. *Japanese manners and ethics in business* (Tokyo: East Asia Publishing Co.), 1963.
26. Doi, T. *The anatomy of dependence* (Tokyo-New York-San Francisco: (Kodansha Int. Ltd.), 1973.
27. —Some psychological themas in Japanese human relationships. In: Condon, J. C. and Saito M. *Intercultural Encounters with Japan* (Tokyo: the Simul Press), 1974.
28. Dore, R. P. *City Life in Japan: a study of a Tokyo ward* (Berkeley: University of California Press), 1965.
29. —ed. *Aspects of Social Change in Modern Japan* (Princeton, N.J.: Princeton University Press), 1967.
30. *British factory—Japanese factory* (Berkeley: University of California Press), 1973.
31. Evans, Jr., R. *The labor economics of Japan and the United States* (New York-Washington-London: Praeger Publishers), 1971.
32. Fairbank, J. K., Reischauer, E. O., and Craig, A. M. *East Asia: The modern transformation* (Boston: Houghton-Mifflin), 1965.
33. Fukutake, T. *Man and society in Japan* (Tokyo: Tokyo University Press), 1963.
34. Furstenberg, F. *Why the Japanese have been so successful in business* (London: Leviathan House), 1974.
35. Gould, R. *The Matsushita phenomenon* (Tokyo: Diamond Sha), 1970.
36. Guillain, R. *The Japanese challenge* (London: Hamish Hamilton), 1970.
37. Hall, J. W., and Beardsley, R. K. *Twelf doors to Japan* (New York etc.: McGraw Hill), 1965.
38. Halloran, R. *Japan: Images and realities* (Tokyo: Tuttle Co.), 1969.
39. Hasegawa, N. *The Japanese character: a cultural profile* (Tokyo: Kodansha Int. Ltd.), 1966.
40. Hayashi, C. Aoyama, H., Nishihira, S., and Suzuki, T. A study of Japanese national character, volume 2. In: *Nipponjin no Kokuminsei (2)* (Tokyo: Shiseido), 1970, pp. 509-569.
41. Hearn, L. *Exotics and retrospectives* (London: Kegan Paul, Trench, Trubner & Co.), 1905.
42. Hirschmeier, J. *The origins of enterpreneurship in Meiji Japan* (Cambridge, Mass.: Harvard University Press), 1964.
43. Ishino, I. Motivational factors in a Japanese labor supply organization. In: *Human Organization,* vol. 15, no. 2, summer 1956.
44. Jansen, M. B. ed. *Changing Japanese attitudes toward modernization* (Princeton, N.J.: Princeton University Press), 1965.
45. *Japan Labour Bulletin:* monthly publication issued by the Japan Institute of Labour.
46. Kahn, H. *The emerging Japanese superstate: challenge and response* (Englewood Cliffs, N.J.: Prentice Hall), 1970.
47. Lebra T. S.: *Japanese patterns of behavior* (Honolulu: University of Hawaii), 1976.
48. Lebra T. A. and Lebra W. P. eds. *Japanese culture and behavior: selected readings* (Honolulu: University Press of Hawaii), 1974.
49. Levine, S. B. *Industrial relations in postwar Japan* (Urbana, Ill.: University of Illinois Press), 1958.
50. Lockwood, W. W. ed. *The state and economic enterprise in Japan* (Princeton, N.J.: Princeton University Press), 1965.
51. Lockwood, W. W. *The economic development of Japan: growth and structural change* (Princeton, N.J.: Princeton University Press), 1968.
52. Mahler, I. 'What is the self concept in Japan?' In: *Psychologia,* vol. 19. 1976, 127-33.
53. Marsh, R. M. and Mannari, H. *Modernization and the Japanese factory* (Princeton, N.J.: Princeton University Press), 1976.
54. Maruyama, M. *Thought and behaviour in modern Japanese politics (Expanded edition)* (London-Oxford-New York: Oxford University Press), 1969.
55. Ministry of Health and Welfare, Japanese Government, *Health and welfare services in Japan* (Tokyo, 1977).
56. Ministry of Labour of the Japanese Government *Yearbook of labour statistics* (Published annually, since 1949).
57. Moore, Ch. A. ed. *The Japanese mind; essentials of Japanese philosophy and culture* (Honolulu: East-West Center Press), 1967.

58. Murakami, H. and Harper, T. J. eds. *Great historical figures of Japan* (Tokyo : The Japan Culture Institute), 1978.
59. Nagai M. (translated by Dusenbury J.) *Higher education in Japan: its take-off and crash* (Tokyo: University of Tokyo Press), 1971.
60. Nakamura, H. *Ways of thinking of eastern peoples: India, China, Tibet, Japan;* revised edition by Wiener, Ph. (Honolulu: East-West Center Press), 1966.
61. Nakane, Chie *Kinship and economic organization in rural Japan* (London: University of London, Athlone Press), 1967.
62. —*Japanese society* (London: Weidenfeld and Nicolson), 1970; also in somewhat revised edition: Pelican Books, 1974.
63. —: The social system reflected in interpersonal communication. In: Condon J. C. and Saito M., eds. *Intercultural encounters with Japan* (Tokyo: The Simul Press), 1974.
64. Nishimoto M. *The development of educational broadcasting in Japan* (Tokyo: Sophia University), 1969.
65. Nijland, E. *Japan en de Japanneezen* (Nijkerk: Callenbach), 1902.
66. Odaka, J. and Nishihira, S. Social mobility in Japan: a report on the 1955 survey of social stratification and social mobility in Japan. *East Asian Cultural Studies,* volume 4, no. 14, March 1965.
67. Okochi, K., Karsh, B. and Levine, S. B. eds. *Workers and employers in Japan: the Japanese employment relations system* (Princeton, N.J.: Princeton University Press), 1973.
68. Ono, T. *Wage problems and industrial relations in Japan* (Tokyo: The Japan Institute of Labour), 1971.
69. Patrick, H. and Meissner, L., eds. *Japanese industrialization and its social consequences* (Berkeley: University of California Press), 1976.
70. Reischauer, E. O. *Japan: past and present* (London: Gerald Duckworth & Co. Ltd.), 1964.
71. —*The Japanese* (Cambridge, Mass.: Harvard Business Press), 1977.
72. Riesman, D. and Riesman, E. T. *Conversations in Japan: modernization, politics and culture* (New York: basic books), 1967.
73. Rohlen, Th. P. Seishin kyoiku in a Japanese bank: a description of methods and consideration of some underlying concepts. *Newsletter of the Council on Anthropology and Education,* volume 2, no. 1, 1971.
74. Sansom, G. B. *The Western world and Japan: a study in the interaction of European and Asiatic cultures* (New York: Vintage Books), 1973.
75. —*A history of Japan (3 volumes)* (originally published by Stanford University Press, 1958-1963) new edition (Tokyo: Tuttle Co., 1974).
76. Smith, Th. C. *The agrarian origins of modern Japan* (Stanford, Cal.: Stanford University Press), 1959.
77. Social Insurance Agency of the Japanese Government *Outline of social insurance in Japan, 1977* (Tokyo: 1977).
78. *This is Sohyo: Japanese workers and their struggles* (Tokyo: Sohyo), 1976.
79. Storry, R., *A history of modern Japan* (London: Penguin Books), 1960.
80. Sueno A. *Entrepreneur and gentleman: a case history of a Japanese company* (Tokyo: Tuttle Co., Ltd.), 1977.
81. Taira, K. *Economic development and the labor market in Japan* (New York-London: Columbia University Press), 1970.
82. Takezawa, S. Changing worker values and policy implications in Japan. In: Davis, L. E. and Cherns, A. B. eds. *The quality of working life, volume 1* (New York: the Free Press), 1975.
83. —The quality of working life: trends in Japan. In: *Labour and Society,* volume 1, no, 1, January 1976 (published by the International Institute for Labour Studies, Geneva).
84. —*Productivity, quality of working life and labour management relations (Productivity Series No. 12)* (Tokyo: Asian Productivity Organization), 1976.
85. —Gewerkschaften und Unternehmungsfuhrung in Japan. In: Ichihara, K. and Takamiya, S. *Die Japanische Unternehmung* (Westdeutscher Verlag), 1977.
86. Tsuda, M. *The basic structure of Japanese labor relations* (Tokyo: Musashi University), 1965.
87. Tsurumi, K. *Social change and the individual: Japan before and after defeat in World War II* (Princeton, N.J.: Princeton University Press), 1970.

158

88.   Van Helvoort, E. J. *Japen's eigen aard* (Den Haag : Informatief no. 6-7, Stichting Maatschappij en Onderneming), 1974.
89.   —Japan : maatschappij en medezeggenschap in het bedrijf. In : *Intermediair*, vol. 10, no. 30, July 26, 1974.
90.   —Dragstra, H. and van Elferen, J. *Werken in Japan* (Assen : van Gorcum & Com. B.V.), 1975.
91.   Van Helvoort, E. J. *Blue-collar workers in Japan and Holland : a comparative study* (Meppel, Holland), 1977.
92.   Vogel, E. F. *Japan's new middle class* (Berkeley-Los Angeles-London : University of California Press ; second edition), 1971.
93.   —ed. *Modern Japanese organization and decision-making* (Berkeley-Los Angeles-London : University of California Press), 1975.
94.   Whitehill, A. M. and Takezawa, S. *The other worker : a comparative study of industrial relations in the United States and Japan* (Honolulu : East-West Center Press), 1968.
95.   Yoshino, M. Y. *Japan's managerial system : tradition and innovation* (Cambridge, Mass.: M.I.T. Press), 1968.
96.   Yoshino. M. Y. *The Japanese marketing system : adaptations and innovations* (Cambridge, Mass : M.I.T. Press), 1971.